My Life in a BLUE SUIT

Making Waves

The real lives of sporting heroes on, in & under the water

My Life in a BLUE SUIT

Jim Saltonstall MBE QP*

(* Queen's Peasant)

FERNHURST
BOOKS

Published in 2023 by Fernhurst Books Limited

The Windmill, Mill Lane, Harbury, Leamington Spa, Warwickshire, CV33 9HP,
UK Tel: +44 (0) 1926 337488 | www.fernhurstbooks.com

A catalogue record for this book is available from the British Library
ISBN 9781912621613

Front cover photograph: Barry Pickthall / PPL
Back cover photograph: Peter Bentley / PPL
Plate section: Saltonstall family archive

Designed & typeset by Daniel Stephen
Printed in India by Replika Press Pvt Ltd

Contents

As rumour has it
olympics
charismatic
medal
compass work
queen's peasant
methodological approach
captivating
coach
positive
yorkshire
belonging
racing rules
up a drainpipe
starting
british
bridlington
boat handling
producing resultss
knowledge
ferret
patriot
sailing
fantastic influence
passion
enthusiasm
her majesty
medallist
inspiration
tactics
queen & country
RYA
confidence
belief
olympic
coiled spring
boat tuning
boat preparation
royal navy
legend
gold medal
meteorology
olympic success
stand out coach
sense of humour
ambition
work ethic
race strategy
british success
incredible character
To cut a short story long
self preparation

Words associated with Jim Saltonstall

Foreword

Team GB currently tops the all-time Olympic sailing medal table with more medals won than any other nation. More specifically, at five out of the last six Olympic Games the team has been the top nation in sailing.

This has been achieved with strong leadership from the Royal Yachting Association and very talented sailors and coaches. In no way could this success be put down to one person, but Barry Pickthall, formerly the Yachting Correspondent of *The Times*, observed:

"If one man deserves recognition for Britain's remarkable success within the sailing Olympic arena, it is Jim Saltonstall – the coach who has cajoled, encouraged and inspired so many youngsters towards world stardom over the past 3 decades."

Rather than a traditional Foreword to this book, we felt it best to leave it to many of the Olympic medallists who have worked with Jim to have their say. In alphabetical order:

Sir Ben Ainslie CBE (Gold medallist 2000, 2004, 2008, 2012, silver medallist 1996):
"Jim inspired generations of World Champions and Olympic medallists. He gave youngsters the belief that they could win, then provided the platform to create the skill sets to get the job done. There are a handful of people who deserve immense credit for the success of British sailing in the last 40 years and Jim is without doubt one of them."

Ian Barker (Silver medallist 2000):
"Jim has been an ever-present in my sailing career. From the first time I attended a talk he was giving as a 14-year-old (me, not him), to being coached at youth level, through 505s, 49ers and then eventually advising me on a transition into coaching. Although he never coached me for any period of time as he did for many of the other contributors, that didn't matter, because what Jim bought to the table more than anything was a method of approaching one's sailing that could be applied to any standard, any class and any sailor who followed it. 'And you don't need me to tell you', it produced results, big ones."

Andy Beadsworth (Youth World Champion 1985, Olympian 1996, 2000, twice Dragon World Champion):
"As a kid I sailed an Optimist, while my parents sailed a Fireball. It was by chance in 1979 that we saw an advert for the 'Youth Squad'. My dad applied and I was accepted for a trial: I was a bit young, but bigger than the average 12-year-old. My life of adventure, a lot of press up, and some success as a 'Ferret' under the 'Queen's Peasant's guidance began and also a lifelong friendship. Having won a number of World Championships now with Jim, my first being the World Youth Championships, along with many others, I owe a lot to him and his vision, drive, determination and immense enthusiasm to excel on the sailing world stage.

What an incredible opportunity it's been. An emphasis on hard work but so much fun!! Maybe occasionally ill advised…

Many of his squad have gone on to win World, European and Olympic Championships in many different classes helping make Team GB and British sailors the best in the world today.

It's been a privilege and an honour to have been involved.

I doubt anyone who's met him has ever forgotten the experience.

Thanks to the Queen, Yorkshire and you 'me old mucker, me old mate'!!"

Stuart Childerley (Youth World Champion 1984, Olympian 1988, 1992, twice Etchell World Champion):
"The sport of sailing has been hugely enhanced for many because of Jim Saltonstall's personality and the youth and ladies' training programme that was established through the RYA (Royal Yachting Association). Those of us who were privileged to work with Jim quickly realised the potential in developing our sailing skills, results and enjoyment of the sport. Jim's ability to motivate sailors to train, practice and perfect their skills was spellbounding. Jim had a unique way of connecting and working with sailors of all ages and experiences. I remember observing Jim run a debrief for a group of soggy, tired and intent youngsters, in which he would always identify the good in everyone while managing to find some humour."

Saskia Clark MBE (Gold medallist 2016, silver medallist 2012):
"The performance record of the athletes that Jim coached is a clear testament to his skills. He created an amazing atmosphere of camaraderie, competitiveness and ambition which kept us all coming back to the water weekend after weekend. He's an absolute legend."

Mark Covell (Silver medallist 2000):
"Every time you meet Jim, he would raise your spirits. He would tell you that Her Majesty sends Her regards and expects great things from you. How could you not hike harder with that patriotic spring in your step. Coaching isn't all about the data and the technology, it's about motivation too. Who knew a Yorkshire boy telling it like it is, could be such a powerful weapon. Long live Jim and the King!"

Chris Draper (Bronze medallist 2004):
"Jim is the most captivating and charismatic person I've been lucky enough to meet. From the youngest to the most decorated athletes, his ability to capture and inspire everyone around him is unmatched. The guidance, values and work ethic Jim installed in all the sailors over the years have, without doubt, been the single most prolific catalyst in Great Britain's success as an Olympic sailing nation. An incredible character who has been such a fantastic influence on every person he's ever worked with."

Dylan Fletcher MBE (Gold medallist 2020):
"From reading his books to then meeting Jim for the first time, he was a huge inspiration and incredibly talented coach. Learning about Johnny and the perfect hill stuck with me throughout my career and always brought me back to my home club and his wise words. His ability to motivate yet push you harder than ever was a true talent and something all coaches strive for. What an all-time great coach that helped countless World and Olympic Champions."

Joe Glanfield (Silver medallist 2004, 2008):
"Jim has a special character and is an incredibly inspiring coach; as a youth he made you want to represent your country, do your best to win and love the challenge sailing offers. He had a fantastic ability as a coach to keep it simple, get you focussing on what mattered within such a complex sport. I was coached by Jim between 16 and 18 years old; by the end of that period, I knew I wanted to go on and try to get to an Olympics; he helped me believe I could do that and make the commitment. I don't think it is any coincidence that so many youth sailors Jim coached went on to excel in the sport."

Paul Goodison MBE (Gold medallist 2008):
"Jim is a one of the stand-out coaches and mentors that deserves great credit for the influence he has had over Britain's success in sailing. His enthusiasm, knowledge and tremendous sense of humour inspired so many young sailors to great things. He was immensely proud of his 'ferrets' and always had time for each and every one of us."

Sarah Gosling OBE (nee Webb) (Gold medallist 2004, 2008):
"I still remember the day I received a letter from Jim, The Queen's Peasant, as he called himself, to say that I had been selected to be part of the National Optimist Squad – aged 12 – I had MADE IT!

Jim's greatest skill was in making us all want to feel part of his gang and being in that gang meant we gave our best at all times. Five of the sailors that received the same letter I refer to are still involved in sailing, this is testament to the work ethic and the love of the sport and the sea that Jim instilled in all of us. Jim built a team of achievers: our gang went on to win 15 Olympic medals. We were never late or we were given press ups and I was regularly told I shouldn't be going around the windward mark discussing the square root of a bleedin' biscuit tin, he was always to be seen with a Yorkie bar…"

Simon Hiscocks (Silver medallist 2000, bronze medallist 2004):
"It is hard not to be influenced by someone with the natural air of confidence and positive spirit that Jim brings along. On reflection he says very little but there is some magic in that little and there are many ferrets with plenty of little in them."

Pippa Kenton-Page MBE (nee Wilson) (Gold medallist 2008):
"It still feels like yesterday I was sitting in a coaching session with Jim, 'like a coiled spring' learning from his passion and enthusiasm for our sport and preparing to sail my socks off for Queen and countrymen. His outstanding ability to ignite passion, empower and educate how to perform in sailing is a rare find. A true pioneer of coaching in British sailing, Jim has continued to lead generations of sailors to victory, and his catchphrases will stay with us for life!"

Luke Patience (Silver medallist 2012):
"I knew Jim before I met him, as his reputation proceeds him! He instilled passion and simplicity in my approach to this wonderful sport and reminded me all along the way that we do this for a greater purpose – the country. He's been present at the start of my journey as a wee kid, right through to 3 Olympic Games. There's a piece of him in my Olympic medal, thank you Jim."

Iain Percy OBE (Gold medallist 2000, 2008, silver medallist 2012):
"Jim Saltonstall was central to and the force behind the great success of the British Olympic Sailing Teams for over two decades. Jim was always fun to be around. He wouldn't have necessarily passed all the modern-day parental laws, but in good way, because he treated his sailors with trust and respect. By giving that responsibility to the Youth Squad sailors he opened their eyes to the realisation that it was their life to define: their efforts would make the difference, and their mistakes would be their undoing. It was a great life lesson he gave to all that came under his guidance; one of many lessons he gave, on sailing and life, that together were the makings of a generation of winning sailors."

Shirley Robertson OBE (Gold medallist 2000, 2004):
"In an extraordinary career, Jim set the foundations of the UK's sailing talent for decades, his analytical approach to training and talent nurturing was the envy of sailing federations around the World. Without doubt he's responsible for Britain's incredible success on the Olympic stage and beyond.........proud to be one of his 'ferrets'.......thanks Jim!"

Nick Rogers (Silver medallist 2004, 2008):
"Nobody is more positive than Jim! Jim created the British Sailing Team's belief that we could win. He is the greatest motivator and team builder. The differences at youth and Olympic level are small and, at some point, you have to believe you can and are going to win. He was such a legend and fun too, I remember he had his birthday at the Optimist Worlds so Ben [Ainslie], Chris [Draper] and I poured a dustbin of ice over him in bed to wake him up! He thought it was hilarious! He was ahead of his time, kind, fun and positive. What more do you need in a leader?"

Giles Scott MBE (Gold medallist 2016, 2020):
"Jim is unique and a fountain of knowledge when it comes to racing. As a 13/14-year-old I couldn't help but be motivated by the delivery of his coaching sessions. Being 'off like a ferret up a drainpipe' in my Topper, and to be headed home from events 'with a medal between my port and starboard nipple' was always goal number one."

Ian Walker (Silver medallist 1996, 2000):
"Jim was ahead of his time in bringing together the best youth talent and giving them a structured approach in order to develop their sailing skills. His real skill was not what he coached, but it was making them feel that they belonged to something special, making them proud to represent Great Britain and in time helping us all believe we could win. You will never meet a more patriotic person."

I must thank Christine most sincerely for all her hard work and hours spent on the computer putting together this project and translating my 'Yorkshire-speak' into the King's English.

Introduction

I began writing this book some time ago whilst cruising in the Red Sea which was quite an accomplishment because, having served 15 years in the Royal Navy, I always maintained that you would never catch me cruising. However, as we all know, 'never say never!' because our son Jeremy's Merchant Naval career had put him in the employ of Carnival UK and serving on Cunard and P&O cruise ships and it was inevitable that I would be expected to do at least one cruise whilst he was on board. So that is how I came to be aboard the MV *Aurora* heading towards the Suez Canal.

I had commented to my wife Christine that I wasn't sure how I would fill up my time and she suggested that I should take my laptop with me and start to write about the many incidents that I had encountered during my life thus far and so it began. Here we are ten years on and, partly thanks to the 'pandemic lockdown' I have at last completed it.

I have thoroughly enjoyed recalling the many aspects of my life and am grateful to all those who, along the way, have helped and encouraged me towards the successes I have achieved. I have also made many friends and shared laughter, fun and occasional mishaps with them. It has been a great journey and I still maintain that if I had to live my life all over again I would not wish to change a thing.

Jim Saltonstall
January 2023

*A young lad asked me why I called them 'ferrets',
to which I replied, because like a ferret you are
very intelligent and very fast like 'ferrets up a
drainpipe'.*

Chapter 1

My Early Years

At a very early age, my life revolved around the water as home for me was Bridlington on the east coast of Yorkshire which was a lovely seaside town with a thriving fishing industry and a very pleasant bay, perfect for sailing, with a very active yacht club, the Royal Yorkshire Yacht Club. I arrived on 22 July 1947 at the Avenue Hospital in Bridlington Old Town, thereby designating me a 'Yorkshireman'.

I will never forget what my mother said to me when I was a child. She said, "Jim lad, in the big scale of things you are only going to be on this planet for a very small percentage of time, so make sure that it is one long permanent holiday", and that is exactly what it has been: one long, permanent holiday! If I had my life to live again, I would not change one thing. I have been very lucky and have generally been in the right place at the right time, which is what life is all about, especially on the starting line; being like a chess player: always thinking ahead, so that you are never in the wrong place at the wrong time!

My parents met at the end of World War Two in Holland. Dad was a Petty Officer shipwright in the Royal Navy and received a King's commendation for his work whilst serving during the war. My mother survived the blitz in Rotterdam and returned to the UK with dad to settle down in Bridlington.

Mum could not speak a word of English, had no friends, but very quickly picked up the Yorkshire language and over the years made many friends. She spoke a little Italian and thankfully there was an Italian ex prisoner of war who ran the local greengrocers, so she managed to do her shopping by communicating with him.

Dad was a master yacht builder and settled down in Bridlington building and repairing yachts. His brains were in his hands, his skill in handling wood and creating some really nice yachts was absolutely awesome. Not only was he a top shipwright, he was also, in his own right, a top class racing helmsman winning many races out of the Royal Yorkshire Yacht Club.

I was christened in the Royal Yorkshire Yacht Club bar by a real character in our sport by the name of Peter Freemantle with a soda siphon which he grabbed from behind the bar. From there I was taken straight down to the harbour, put on to a Yorkshire One Design *Iolanthe* and had my first sail – so I guess I was destined to be a seafarer at some stage in my life.

Looking back on my early days on the planet, I was very lucky to get past my first winter as it was the coldest on record. The windows froze on the inside, the snow lasted well into March with snow drifts five metres high and there was no such thing as central heating and no thermal wear available to us in those days.

Our first home was a flat on the south side of town and eventually mum and dad managed to obtain a newly built three-bedroomed council house, number 17 Wright Crescent, built on an estate called West Hill to house the population recovering from the Second World War. These houses were family houses so there were plenty of other children, and quite a few 'tearaways' to play with whilst growing up.

My life was soon to become ever more hectic with the arrival of two brothers Richard (Dick) followed by Antony (Podge). There was just over a year between Dick and myself and five years between me and Antony. I know we were a handful for mum especially when Dick and I would gang up against Antony who suffered a great deal from us whilst growing up, being the youngest, and the target of much mischief.

I remember on one occasion Dick and I emptied a bag of flour over Antony whilst he was lying in his cot and all you could see were his little eyes peering through. On another occasion mum could hear what she thought was Dick and I playing table tennis but when she came upstairs to have a look we were using eggs instead of a ping pong ball! What we didn't appreciate of course was that eggs were rationed at that time, and we had probably wasted a week's egg ration! Our punishment for misbehaving was a smack with the dreaded *mattaclopper* (Dutch for carpet beater!!).

Our house had a large garden backing on to a wooded area with very large oak trees running along the main road out of Bridlington: a great place for hide and seek and building dens. Dick and I would climb to the top of one of the tallest trees for a fantastic view over Bridlington and out over the bay. For fun we would take with us a loud bell which we would ring as loud as we could, much to the annoyance of the neighbours. Mum went absolutely ballistic when we eventually came down: we knew we would receive another whack from the infamous *mattaclopper*, and boy did it hurt! We never learnt!

Mum told us that whenever she needed to catch the bus to return home from town, in order to prevent one of us from running off, she would carry one under each arm and place the third in a litter bin which was fastened to the side of the bus stop. She would then deposit two in the bus and go back for the third! The bus driver saw the funny side of this and would just wait for her to climb aboard with her brood.

My grandmother still lived in Rotterdam in Holland in a lovely old three-storey terraced house, and we visited her often. We always looked forward to these visits as she usually spoilt us rotten. On one visit mum had handmade new coats for all three of us for the trip. We were all dressed up ready to go when I decided I would have one last play in our recently acquired toy pedal car. What I did not know was that dad had just given it a fresh lick of red paint, so you can imagine what I looked like when I climbed out as my new coat was covered in it. Mum broke down in tears and once again out came the *mattaclopper*!

We would travel on the North Sea Ferries either the *Melrose Abbey* or the *Bolton Abbey* and on one of these journeys we snuck out on deck to play. When a steward came looking for us he found Dick and I holding on to Antony's legs, dangling him over the stern of the ship for a laugh. We were in big trouble that time! It's no wonder that Antony's hair turned grey at a young age when you know what he endured as the youngest in the family. At one time he was mistaken for my father – that made my day!

We grew up to be very independent and I remember, as a young lad, walking down to the bus stop and getting on to the bus, climbing upstairs and sitting in the front seat. As I was so small my head came below the top of the seat, so when the conductor looked through the downstairs mirror to see if there were any passengers upstairs, he could not see me. I sat there all the way into town enjoying the view until I reached the bus station. Fortunately for me the driver was Mr Bell who was our next-door neighbour; he recognised me as I stepped off the bus and he grabbed me by the collar and took me back home on the next bus.

As three young ferrets we actually got on really well together and with dad working down on the harbour, my brothers and I spent all our spare time there messing about in any boat we could find. If there were no boats available, we would find a wooden fish box or anything that would stay afloat and drag it into the water and skull around the harbour.

Our dad was an excellent sailor as well as being a shipwright and on occasions he would do some yacht deliveries, mainly to and from the south coast. On one occasion he had to deliver a yacht called *Deborah* to the south coast and decided to take me with him as an extra hand along with Paddy McCarthy. I was about nine years old and very excited to be going on this great adventure. As we progressed south passing Cromer the weather started to take a turn for the worse and we were caught up in a full-on gale.

I was beginning to feel seasick and, as I dashed below to the heads, I realised that I wasn't going to make it when I spotted the large pan on the stove which we used for cooking dinner. As it was nearer than the heads, I proceeded to be sick in it. Only then did I realise that the pan already contained our on-going pot mess which was added to every day. We finally made it into Yarmouth and, after securing alongside and tidying up, both my dad and Paddy sat down for a well-deserved hot meal and tucked into the pot mess. Thankfully I could claim to have lost my appetite due to sea sickness and never said a word, but they both seemed to enjoy it!

Soon we were being taken out sailing, usually in the local class of boat, the Yorkshire One Design, which originated in 1847. There are still a few racing in the bay today having been cherished and in some cases restored. One of dad's friends, Ken Shippey, used to take us out in the early days, teaching us the basics of seamanship and how to sail, so we learnt a great deal from the pair of them. We would be out in all conditions in our woolly jumpers, soaked to the skin, no oilskins in those days, every finger a marlin spike!!!

Soon the time came for me to start helming, then shortly after to start racing. As Bridlington is on the east coast it can experience some very rough weather, so the sailing season is relatively short – April through to the end of September – so we had much to learn in a short time. I took to this like a duck to water and thereafter most weekends and school holidays were spent sailing on anybody's yacht that had a crew vacancy.

My school days started at Hilderthorpe School; I was never really interested in lessons and plodded through them along with all the other children. I cannot say that I particularly enjoyed or disliked school, it was just something you had to do. I certainly did not excel in any subject – I was sort of 'middle of the road', only putting in enough effort to get by and not upset the teachers too much!

It was there that I met Chris Wright. We were in the same class, and both had the same attitude to schooling so naturally became best friends. His dad was part owner of the *Bridlington Queen*, one of the pleasure boats in the harbour taking holidaymakers out around the bay, and so we were regularly down at the harbour together. We often skipped school and took off down to the harbour to lark about and usually got a clip around the ear from the local fishermen for getting in their way. Many years later, Chris became the Harbour Master: what goes around comes around, he could now take charge of the local truants – no clip around the ear nowadays though!

The time arrived when Dick and I were being called upon to crew for some of the top sailors in the club, racing in the new Dragon class which was developing on the east coast of Yorkshire. John Rix, who owned a boat called *Monatoo* – DK 308, asked me to be his bowman with his uncle Les in the middle of the boat. Dick crewed for Heather & Rosemary Smailes on *Karen* – DK304. They were sisters who were both very determined to do well in the sport, and they did, winning on many occasions. I spent four very happy years racing on *Monatoo*, learning a lot from both John and Les Rix. What I learnt from them and my father was to set me up for my future racing career on both the national and the international stage of yacht and dinghy racing.

When I was eleven, I failed my eleven plus and moved on to St Georges Secondary Modern School for Boys. It was a very good school with good teachers, the best of which was my last class teacher, Mr Johnny Walker. He was strict but had a sense of humour; if he thought that you were not paying attention in class, he would throw the blackboard rubber at you and he had a very good aim and, boy, did it hurt!

It was becoming clear that I was not going to be an academic ferret, perhaps because I played truant so often, and did not pass any exams. I left school without any qualifications (unlike my two brothers who 'hoovered' up numerous 'A' and 'O' levels between them) but thankfully my attitude changed when I joined the Royal Navy when I was usually one of the top three in the class and progressed through the ranks very rapidly.

Mum and dad got divorced when I was around 14 years old, and times were hard for mum, looking after three hooligans and taking on various jobs in order to pay the rent. To help out, Dick and I did two paper rounds each day and at weekends for Mr Garland, a local newsagent in Bridlington. Omi, our grandmother, gave both Dick and me a Raleigh bicycle each. They were great bikes, large 'sit up and beg' ones, we did a lot of miles on them doing our paper rounds and cycling to school and back. I also cycled to Hull and back with Bruce Beswick, a school friend of mine; we must have been bonkers as it was nearly 30 miles each way, we were pretty shattered when we arrived home.

Chapter 2

Starting In The Navy

Being so involved with the sea, and to make life easier for mum, at the ripe old age of 15 I decided that it was time follow in my father's footsteps and join the Royal Navy as there was no future for me in Bridlington. So I applied and passed all the basic tests. A minimum height was required to be accepted into the Royal Navy and I didn't reach it. However, the officer who was interviewing me said "stand on your tiptoes lad", held up the measure and told me I was in!

Mum took me down to the Bridlington railway station and I boarded the train for London. I had one small suitcase, as I would be 'kitted out' when I arrived. Mum had packed me some sandwiches, an apple and a Blue Riband biscuit. I sat in a compartment and watched the world go by as I journeyed south to a completely new life.

When I arrived in Kings Cross, I walked to Liverpool Street Station from where I caught the train to Ipswich. (I had never been on the Underground and didn't fancy it!) I met up with other lads who were also joining HMS *Ganges* and we were put on to a blue Royal Navy bus and taken to our destination. I was four foot eleven inches tall, weighing in at seven stone – ready to become a trained killer!

What a life changing experience this was going to be! After only one day at HMS *Ganges*, my hair had never been so short, and my shoes had never been so highly polished! HMS *Ganges* was the basic Royal Navy training school at Shotley on the River

Stour / Orwell peninsula. It was to be twelve months of basic training.

I joined in November 1962 as a junior seaman, 54 Recruitment, Collingwood Division, 36 Mess, situated under the short, covered way and my official number was P/070223F, being paid 15 shillings a week (75 pence in today's money). It was very similar to the scenes in the 1960's television series about Stalag 17! There were 20 beds on each side of the hut on a wooden floor which we had to keep clean. We regularly had to form a line and get down on our hands and knees and move backwards slowly, polishing the floor with hand brushes as we went. It was a very long floor! When we had finished, it looked like a mirror but if our Divisional Officer was not happy with it we had to do it all over again!

What an experience that was. Looking back on it now, with all the hardships and discomforts a faint memory, it was absolutely great. I really enjoyed the experience, and it went by in a flash as we were kept so busy, working and training from five o'clock in the morning until ten o'clock at night, six days a week. In no time it was all over, and we were off to our next training phase.

If ever there was a time when I regretted having three initials and a long surname it was whilst I was serving at HMS *Ganges*. One of our first tasks was to hand sew our name into every item of our kit using red silk. As you can well imagine, it took me the best part of my time at *Ganges* to complete it all. Thankfully once we left our basic training we were no longer expected to do this which was quite a relief!

During my time at *Ganges*, all my spare time was spent out on the river sailing 32-foot cutters or 27-foot whalers. I soon acquired my first-class coxswain's badge and was winning races, which led me to representing *Ganges* at various sailing events, leading to me getting my *Ganges* colours as a top-class racing ferret!

For those of you who don't know, HMS *Ganges* had a ship's

mast which was used for training: it was 143 feet high, with three main yard arms. You were allowed to climb it whenever you wished and, during quiet moments (which were rare), I would climb the mast and sit on the half moon and write postcards to my mum. There was a cracking view overlooking both Felixstowe and Harwich! It didn't take me long to get up there as I was like a ferret up a drainpipe, but you did have to hold on tight up there though! Unfortunately, a young rating had fallen off shortly before we arrived, bouncing off the safety net and falling through the post office roof.

The winter of 1962/63 was a repeat of 1947, the 'beast from the east' which lasted for over three months. Everything within *Ganges* froze, including the heating because all the pipes burst; both the rivers Stour & Orwell were completely frozen so there was no sailing or boat drills. *Ganges* was cut off by five-metre snowdrifts on numerous occasions and life was a struggle for all. As there was no heating in the messes, we would go about wearing a towel around our heads in order to keep warm as it was so bitterly cold.

I reached the dizzy heights of Petty Officer Junior, taking charge of our mess and various other duties. One night I led a night raid on the mess next door which turned out to be a mega pillow fight with pillows bursting open and sending feathers everywhere! Unfortunately, we were caught out by a night patrol and, as I recall, the whole mess (40 of us) were made to march around the parade ground until one o'clock in the morning in our pyjamas, oilskin coats and gas masks. We didn't do it again!

They were great days at *Ganges* even though it was hard work; it was an excellent introduction to a career in the Royal Navy.

Whilst I'm talking about HMS *Ganges*, I must just add that I have attended a couple of reunions which are held over a weekend and very well attended.

The first one I attended with my mates Brian Dunn and Stuart Lawson was like turning the clock back. We had a reunion dinner on the Saturday evening, which was a black-tie occasion with the Second Sea Lord as guest of honour, and afterwards we had a mega 'sods opera' hosted by Shep Woolley. This went on into the early hours with many of us not getting to our beds until daylight only to find that a letter had been posted informing us that we were required to attend Sunday morning Church Parade as the Royal Navy chaplain was concerned that there would be a poor 'turn out'. After only a couple of hours kip we all turned up in our Sunday 'best' for the service only to realise that the letter had been a complete 'wind up' and was signed 'H Nelson'. Well, the 'solids hit the air conditioning' as we tried to identify the culprit! Eventually we saw the funny side of it all and at least the chaplain was 'over the moon' with the attendance!

The last one I went to was a special centenary reunion and on the Sunday morning a march past took place in Ipswich Docks. The Second Sea Lord took the salute, so we all turned up in our best 'bib and tucker'. A serving Master at Arms got us all together and there was approximately 100 of us in four platoons. The Master at Arms called us all to attention in his usual loud voice and then from within the platoon a voice suddenly shouted, "say please!" Well, that did it, all of us were still laughing our heads off whilst we marched past. Then another bright spark shouted, "Right Wheel" which meant all of us should turn right, however, this would have led us all over the edge and into the dock – typical matelot humour!

After my *Ganges* days, I had chosen to be part of the radar / navigation branch and went off to join HMS *Dryad*, which was the School of Navigation, in a small village called Southwick just north of Portsmouth. If I remember correctly, I spent a year there before qualifying as a Junior Seaman Radar Plotter Basic. We then went off to sea on our very first ship, great excitement all round.

I joined HMS *Wakeful*, a Type-15 anti-submarine frigate in Portsmouth in January 1964. She was a good ship with a good ship's company, and I basically travelled all around Europe on her doing anti-submarine exercises and flying the flag for Great Britain. Accommodation was tight as we had approximately 20 matelots in our mess. We slept in hammocks which gave you a good nights' sleep except when the body next to you was getting into or out of his! The other downside was that, as the mess table was below the hammocks, you could be eating your meal when you might get a foot right in the middle of your plate! Happy days.

One of the highlights was that we were involved in the making of the film *The Bedford Incident* which starred Richard Wydmark and Gina Lollobrigida. To our delight they stayed on board for a few days and all the lads were lusting after Gina Lollobrigida. Later the toilet seat which she had sat on was sold for a fortune!

During my time on HMS *Wakeful* I started dinghy sailing which was new to me as we never had any dinghies in Bridlington or during my time at *Ganges*. Learning how to sail in yachts first and then moving into dinghies is not the way to do it. It should have been the other way round as I soon learnt after a few capsizes!!

After a few swims and numerous righting drills, I mastered the art of sailing a Bosun dinghy in a breeze. The Bosun dinghy was chosen as a robust heavy displacement dinghy for Navy sailing which was basically Jack proof! They were used for all the dinghy sail training courses as well as all for racing events, with large numbers in all the shore establishments and on board the ships.

It was not long before I was selected to join the Royal Navy Dinghy Team, and this led to 12 great years of representing the Royal Navy at numerous events against the Army and the Royal Air Force as well as other clubs and organisations. The Royal Navy Dinghy Team in those days (the mid to late sixties and the seventies) had some famous racing ferrets including Rodney Pattisson, David Howlett, Jo Richards, Kevin Podger, Dave Maclean, Richard Aylard, Tom Mason, Tony Belben (Jason Belben's dad), David Lindsey, Peter Colclough and numerous others. We had some great times over the years of competition.

Back then, when we still had a Navy, we were often air lifted by helicopter from the ship out in the southwestern approaches to wherever we were required to represent the Royal Navy in an event and then flown back! Those were the days!

It was around this time in my life when I acquired a scooter, a Lambretta 125cc. I did some serious miles on it around East Yorkshire before taking it down to the south coast by train when I was stationed in Portsmouth. One weekend I decided to ride it all the way back to Bridlington from Pompey – what an epic journey that turned out to be! It took me nine hours and for the last 30 miles I had no brakes left. When I arrived in Bridlington, I couldn't stand up straight for an hour or so. When I took off my goggles, I had big white patches around my eyes where my goggles had protected them from the dirt and all the diesel particles which had stuck to my face during the journey!

After I had recovered a couple of days later, I went up to see a mate of mine who lived near Sunderland and, for some reason, I managed to come off it twice in one day. That was enough for me, I never rode it again after that and passed it on to Antony, who was unfortunately knocked off it, but not seriously hurt, and eventually sold it on. I have never ridden a motorised bike again – too dangerous!

After serving my time aboard HMS *Wakeful* I began to climb through the ranks both as a seaman and as a radar plotter; my first promotion was to an Able Seaman RP3. I was then drafted to join HMS *Decoy* in Portsmouth a Daring class destroyer. However, it soon became obvious that she would never make the deadline for completion of her refit and into deployment to the Far East, so we were transferred to HMS *Delight* in Rosyth Scotland, to drag her out in time.

HMS *Delight* was another great ship with a great crew, and I had a good two and a half years on board her. We had a few hairy moments whilst on her which I will never forget.

We did a tour of the Middle East and cruised through the Red Sea where we anchored off Jeddah. I was on duty as 'boat's crew', my job being the bowman. As we approached the jetty I carried out my boat hook drill, placing the end of the hook onto the jetty to pull us alongside when immediately the shaft became infested with what appeared to be 'hundreds' of cockroaches, heading straight in my direction! Needless to say, I released it from my hands rather fast and watched as it sunk into oblivion. The coxswain was not amused at my action, but that's life!

We were involved in the withdrawal of the British troops from Aden and, although we were not fighting ashore, we experienced a few bullets flying around during our time alongside where we took on board both soldiers and members of the RAF. They say it's a small world and, in my case, this was certainly true because I knew two of the people who we took on board: one of them was my Uncle Jim, a Lieutenant Colonel with the King's Own Yorkshire Regiment, and the other person was my dad's friend Ken Shippey who was with the RAF. It was good to have them on board and catch up on what was going on back home in Bridlington. We headed south and dropped them off in Mombasa from where they travelled back to England.

Having offloaded that lot, we then went on to the conflict in Borneo to stop the gun runners, and again experienced some flying bullets especially during the night. During our passage across the Indian Ocean, I had to visit the heads one night and as I walked in, this body (Pete Harvey) came crashing through a loo door spread eagled across the floor with his shorts around his ankles. When I had picked him up and he had gathered himself together, he explained that a flying fish had come through the wind scoop behind him and landed on the small of his back and frightened the life out of him. Well, we killed ourselves laughing over it.

Wind scoops were essential on a non-air-conditioned ship, especially in that heat; you could fry an egg on the open deck!

They could, however, be a source of trouble and once, on one of the many occasions when we had to refuel at sea, we approached our tanker doing over 20 knots. The Officer of the Watch gave the order "starboard twenty" to the wheelhouse in order to pick up the hose trailing behind the tanker. This was like doing a hand brake turn and the ship listed to one side! No one had given the order to remove the wind scoops and suddenly the Indian Ocean started rushing through the ship because the wind scoops were still out on the lower deck, taking in sea water instead of fresh air! There were sailors flying everywhere! Needless to say, the person responsible received a severe rollicking from the skipper as it took us hours to clean up the mess and dry everything out!

We had earned some rest and recuperation time and we spent it in Singapore, which was amazing for a young Yorkshire lad, so I made the most of it! I celebrated my eighteenth birthday whilst we were there and all my mates on the ship dragged me ashore kicking and screaming! What a night! We ended up in Boogie Street until the early hours of the morning. What an experience that was, the bars, the nightclubs and shows were something else: you could buy and sell anything under the 'moon' (it wasn't open in the daytime!). People from all over the world, and sailors from other ships in port, would gravitate there, so the occasional 'punch up' or beer fight would kick off. Rickshaw races and numerous other activities happened down Boogie Street all night until sunrise. You were told not to go off with a gorgeous looking girl because more often or not 'she' would be a 'he'. The 'lady boys' were quite an attraction there! No wonder it has completely changed now. Unfortunately, whilst staggering back to the ship in the pitch dark I slipped and fell into a monsoon ditch by the side of the road. These were deep drainage ditches full of rubbish and sometimes rats and the occasional dead body! As my mates were ahead of me no one saw me go in and I was left there all night. I woke up in the early hours of the morning staring up into the bright sun with filthy, water up to my chest –

31

not a pretty sight. How I ever lived to tell the tale I don't know.

My mates did try to find me once they realised I was missing but couldn't find me in the dark and half submerged. Thankfully I woke up in time to return on board before the end of leave and luckily the Master of Arms turned a blind eye to the state I was in as I staggered up the gangway. I needed a shower and had to purchase a new uniform!

After Singapore, we moved north up to Hong Kong – what a great city, we had a fabulous time there. We would have some great runs ashore, often renting rickshaws and having races from pub to pub, negotiating some very dangerous corners, usually on only one wheel. To this day I don't know how we survived!

Whilst we were stationed in Hong Kong, during refit, I managed to do a lot of sailing which was good. I even managed to sail Susie's Chinese junk, which was awesome. It was like the 'Tardis', a true junk on the outside but a palace on the inside – absolutely fantastic.

Susie was the boss of Susie's side party, workers who were employed by the Ministry of Defence to paint the ships whilst they were in refit, and she was a very wealthy lady. It was great to catch up with her again when she and some of her side party were invited to London to open the Boat Show at Earls Court. We were sad to leave as we moved on making our way back to the UK via the Suez Canal.

My next promotion was to Leading Seaman RP2, and more experiences ensued. One of them was when we were rounding the Isles of Scilly on our return from Scotland to Plymouth for our Easter leave in 1967. The oil tanker, *Torrey Canyon*, had run aground off the Isles of Scilly at that time and was leaking oil into the sea. As we were the first ship at the scene, we were deployed for clean up duties. What a mess! We were there for six weeks, cleaning up the crude oil that had spilled out from her and was covering a vast area of the English Channel. We were in and out of Falmouth collecting detergent which was used to disperse the thick oil. The ship was absolutely covered in the stuff. The stench of crude oil went right through her, and it took weeks to get rid of the smell. The RAF was brought in to bomb the wreck and coincidentally one of the pilots was Barry Wilson who lived four doors away from us in Bridlington. I was able to talk to him over radio, small world isn't it – two lads from Bridlington sorting out the *Torrey Canyon*.

On another occasion I was lucky to survive as a buoy jumper. This involved me getting onto a large mooring buoy to connect a wire hawser to it before then connecting the anchor cable. When I was on the buoy, the ship moved too far away from it and I could sense, as you do, that the wire hawser was straining and about to part, so me and my mate Jimmy Green dived off and swam as fast as we could towards the sea boat. The wire parted and, when that happened, the buoy disappeared under the bow and came out the other side! That was a close one; some sailors have lost limbs and even been killed in that situation. The captain called us to his cabin, apologised and gave us a tot of rum to warm us up – that went down well!

Chapter 3

Moving On In The Navy

My time came to an end on the *Delight*. She was a great ship; we were all sad to leave her and, if I remember rightly, she then went on to be scrapped.

My next deployment was back to HMS *Dryad* to complete my RP2 course which I'm pleased to say I achieved. There were some great lads serving in *Dryad* at that time and we became good mates; brother Dick was also there. We therefore had quite a few social events in and around the village of Southwick, usually in either the Red Lion or the Gold Lion.

The Red Lion was the favourite as Sid, the landlord, would often have a 'lock in' after closing time. On one occasion, after a Saturday lunchtime gathering, we were driving back to *Dryad* and, as we turned a bend, we saw in front of us our mate 'Jumper' Cross in his upside-down car full of sailors. We rushed to help and the first thing I did was kick out the back window to get the lads out. However, 'Jumper' was already out and looked at me and asked me why I did that as it was the only window left intact! He was not a happy 'ferret' but thankfully no one was injured!

I was at HMS *Dryad* until January 1968 when I was then sent to HMS *Bellerophon*, a Naval ship moored alongside in Whale Island, where I passed my Petty Officer's examination. I was promoted to Acting Petty Officer during my time on board my next ship HMS *Phoebe*; a Chatham-based Leander class frigate, which I served on from late 1968 until December 1971.

It was whilst between ships in 1967/68 that my brother Dick

and I found ourselves crewing for a real character by the name of Alex Macleod who owned a Dragon called *Bonaventure*. Alex was from Scotland and worked for the Grants Whisky Company and would tow his Dragon all over Europe with his Ferrari. He had a great sense of humour, and we had some real laughs crewing for him. We never won anything as the boot of the Ferrari was always full of samples of whisky which had to be drunk during the regattas! We had a great time wherever we went; Alex was a very sociable man – a typical Scottish character promoting and selling a lot of whisky on our travels. He arranged for Dick and I to join him to celebrate my 21st birthday at the Haven Hotel in Sandbanks and I can't remember much about it but I know it was a good 'do'!

During this time Christine and I became 'an item' which meant I was travelling up to Bridlington regularly at weekends. Also, my sailing was going from strength to strength, both Captain Norman Fitzgerald and Commander Richardson, who were Navy Sailing Selectors, kept me actively involved in both the Navy Dinghy Team and the Keelboat Team, attending most of the inter-services regattas and team racing. I was still racing in Bridlington during leave and at weekends and I was also crewing with my old mate Peter Freemantle for a guy by the name of Simon Tate on a Dragon called *Royalist*. We were campaigning for the Olympic Games in Germany 1972, and doing very well, as we were amongst the top boats competing for the slot at that time. But, as my time was limited, I was unable to commit to the programme and could not continue with the campaign on *Royalist*, so I had to give up my place to Alistair Curry which was a shame as they were selected to go to the Olympics but 'that's life in a Blue Suit!'

HMS *Phoebe* was to be yet another good ship, a good captain and a good ship's company, and I was in charge of the forecastle. This was also the ship on which I served with my brother Dick and, needless to say, we had a fantastic holiday courtesy of the

British taxpayer! We managed to do a lot of sailing, representing both the ship and the Navy in various places around the world.

Two years we spent on the *Phoebe* under Captain Pritchard, who was an excellent skipper and went on to be an Admiral and became Flag Officer Sea Training at Portland. Little did I know that I would meet him again on my next ship.

My accommodation onboard HMS *Phoebe* was in the after Petty Officer's mess which was amidships and immediately underneath the helicopter flight deck. I had the top bunk which placed me approximately half a metre underneath the helicopter, which was not a pleasant experience during night flight operations when I cursed the fact that we carried a 'paraffin pigeon' on board!

In the Navy on every ship and shore base you serve on, you meet people who become lifelong friends and I made many during my naval career.

There were many happy memories from that commission. We played a few pranks, some of which meant that Dick and I nearly ended up in front of the skipper as defaulters! There was one occasion when we were up in Faslane, Scotland working with an Australian submarine on exercise with our helicopter aloft trying to locate the submarine. The pilot radioed in and said, "Have a look over the transom." On inspection it was discovered that, during the previous night, the Aussies had painted a large green kangaroo on our stern! So, the following night, whilst we were both at anchor in Brodick Bay, we nipped across in the rubber boat and painted a big white moon (which was the *Phoebe*'s crest) on their conning tower.

This sort of banter went on all the time, and we had a great couple of weeks with the Aussies. Other pranks carried out under the influence of alcohol included finding a large smelly camel in Bahrain and trying to bring it back on board, which was not an easy thing to do; and also adopting a Dalmatian dog and taking it on board with us during the early hours of the morning. Firstly, we woke up the lads in our mess in order to introduce the dog to them, and then we put ear defenders on to the dog and took it down to the engine room to meet the stokers. We also took a swan on board to meet its namesake, my mate David Swann! These pranks were not always popular with the rest of the lads!

Whilst we were acting as guard ship in Gibraltar over Christmas and New Year, I was in charge of a patrol craft keeping watch, as there was a dispute going on between the UK and Spain over a stretch of water in the bay outside the harbour. The Spanish Navy decided to anchor one of their ships in this disputed territory in defiance of the UK Government. We couldn't have that so during the night the lads and I nipped out in the rubber boat and hoisted the white ensign on the back end of this Spanish ship; when daylight broke there it was in full view! Well, the 'solids hit the air conditioning': we had caused a big diplomatic incident and an inquiry followed. Sure enough, the finger was pointed at me and I was summoned to the Flag Officer Gibraltar's office to explain. I, as you would expect, received a severe reprimand but, as I walked towards the door, the Admiral said, "By the way Saltonstall, well done!"

At the beginning of March 1970, I said a fond farewell to Christine and set off for a ten-month tour of duty which took us to the Far East via Cape Town.

For several weeks we were involved with the Beira patrol which saw us patrolling the seas off Mombasa to stop supplies reaching Rhodesia, which was a bit of a tedious operation. To pass the time away the 'Beira Bucket' was established: a competition between all the ships involved. This included various games over a set period of time which included volleyball, deck hockey, obstacle courses, tug-of-war and five-a-side football amongst others. The prize, as you will have guessed, was a battered old bucket which I am pleased to say we won during our tour of duty.

We then stopped off in Bahrain, Bombay, Singapore, Hong

Kong, Osaka, Kobe, Yokohama and back home via Cape Town again. Whilst we were in Bahrain, I had the chance to meet up with Christine's brother Norman, who was serving as a navigating officer with Shell Tankers: it's a small world, you are not safe anywhere! It was a strange meeting as he was not allowed out of the security perimeter, so I went round, and we chatted through the fence for an hour or so!

Also, whilst we were in Bahrain, we had plenty of opportunity to sail, so we would take out a Bosun dinghy or a Piccolo, which was basically a surfboard with a 'handkerchief' as a sail for propulsion. One time I was some distance offshore when suddenly I sensed that I was not alone and saw sea snakes with their heads raised up above the water. With only three inches of freeboard, I was not a happy ferret! To add to that, panic stations, a manta ray with a wingspan of approximately three metres appeared and took off flapping its wings and headed straight towards me. It was just as well that I was wearing my brown corduroy swimming trunks! I never sailed the Piccolo again whilst in the Persian Gulf!

After yet another birthday 'run ashore' we staggered back on board the ship's gangway on to the flight deck and it was whilst walking aft, back to the mess, that the birthday boy, Spud Tate who had quite a 'skin full', fell off the flight deck down into the mortar well which was some 15 feet below with a metal deck! We all ran to assist him, thinking the worst, only to see him pick himself up, dust himself down and stagger onward to his mess. I think that if he had been sober, he would have been seriously injured or even dead, but there was not a mark on him. It was absolutely amazing how lucky he was. I suppose it was because his body was so relaxed with the amount of alcohol he had consumed that he bounced when he landed!

One final story, which created a big problem, happened whilst we were in Cape Town on our way home. We had been on this deployment with another frigate, and she was ranked junior to us as we were 'Captain of the Frigate Squadron' and this was demonstrated by a black topped funnel. During our time together she had been given all the rubbish jobs so in protest at night their crew managed to climb on board and they painted the top of our funnel grey and theirs black. This did not go down at all well and it meant that we had to spend a couple of extra days in Cape Town until it was established who had done it and the funnels had been rebranded. This time it was nothing to do with me, I was in the clear!

In 1655 the Royal Navy began the tradition of issuing rum to all sailors and in 1850 they regulated it to a measure of one eighth of a 70ml bottle and it became known as a 'tot' and it was whilst I was on HMS *Phoebe* on 31 July 1970 that this tradition was stopped. 'Tot time' was no more. A sad day!

As we knew it was going to happen, most of the ship's company managed to store up some supplies ready for a big party when we arrived back in the UK in time for Christmas leave. There were bottles everywhere, mainly hidden in the ventilation fan trunkings above our heads. Every time the ship turned you could hear them rolling around and we hoped that they would never be heard by the hierarchy and confiscated! Luckily it was never found, and you have never seen so much rum appear from every nook and cranny when the farewell party got going. All the fan trunkings were emptied, and it was just one big mega party, it was awesome.

On occasions an impromptu party would kick off in the mess. I was in the after Petty Officers' mess and our mess president was a guy by the name of Dave Swann. Dave was the Petty Officer TASI on board in charge of the underwater world, sonar and all things to do with submarines. Dave and I were on opposite watches to each other on the upper deck and one night after one of these parties with beer flying everywhere, off the bulkheads, the deck head, I was a bit under the weather. Unfortunately, I had the middle watch that night – midnight to four in the morning – and, when I arrived for my duty on the bridge, I made myself scarce telling the Officer of the Watch that I was going to do my rounds of the ship because I must have smelt like a brewery! At three o'clock in the morning I couldn't stay awake any longer but, knowing I had another hour to go before Dave came to take over from me and realising I wasn't going to make it, I went below and gave Dave a shake and said, "Come on Dave time for your watch." Of course, Dave didn't think anything about it but when he got up to the bridge, he didn't recognise anyone as it was not his watch! As he looked around, he realised what I had done which meant he had an extra hour on duty! It took him a long time to forgive me for that, although we are still good mates to this very day!! We arrived back into Portsmouth on 16 December 1970 to a great reception and left the ship in Chatham on the 18th and home in time for Christmas.

I had passed my driving test at the age of eighteen, after the fourth time of trying; I failed the first one for speeding, the second one for reversing over the pavement and the third one for driving over a zebra crossing whilst someone stepped onto it! I was a confident driver as I had been driving for months using my brother Dick's licence as there was so little difference in our ages and he had passed his test first time and I had bought my first car which was an 850cc Austin Mini. It was a great little car and was to do some serious mileage between Portsmouth and Bridlington over the years, especially once Christine and I started going out together in 1968.

To help out with the costs, some weekends I would fill it with three fellow matelots and their baggage for the return trip up north (some of these lads were fairly well built as well!). How it did it almost every weekend for a couple of years I'll never know.

Eventually it did blow up on the MI and we had to thumb it home! I couldn't afford to pay 'southern' prices for the repairs so, when Christine had finished work on Saturday morning, I borrowed my mum's little A35 saloon and set off after lunch down the M1 to the Watford Gap Services, where we had abandoned it, to tow the Mini back to Bridlington.

What an epic journey that was! I was in the A35 towing Christine who, after a few hours of using the indicators (I kept pulling out to overtake into the fast lane!) had no power. By this time, it was dark and, as she had no lights, we placed a flashing torch on the back shelf. Then it started to rain, and she had no windscreen wipers, so we had to keep stopping to wipe the windscreen. Then the tow line became disconnected which I didn't notice (and as the horn didn't work, she couldn't attract my attention). Eventually I realised that I was not pulling any weight and had to turn round go back and find her in the middle of a dark country road with no lights, as by this time the torch's battery had gone flat! You can imagine, by the time I reached her she was not a happy ferret!

We eventually got back to Bridlington late that night after at least a 12-hour journey. I left the Mini in Bridlington to be repaired by mum's regular mechanic and took the train back to Pompey. The mini had a reconditioned engine installed which took a couple of weeks to do. When it was ready, I asked Christine to bring it to Chatham as the ship was docked there at the time. She agreed to drive it to her aunts in London for me to pick it up. In those days a reconditioned engine needed a certain amount of 'running in' and therefore she could not go above 40 miles an hour which she said seemed to take forever! I wouldn't have been able to stick at that! That mini was just incredible.

Another car related story happened the year before we were married. We decided to visit Portsmouth to get some idea of the housing market and it just so happened that I had been asked to crew with Peter Freemantle at the weekend in Cowes on the Isle of Wight. In those days the hovercraft left from Southampton, so we crossed the River Itchen on the chain ferry and parked the car in the ferry car park and went over to Cowes. On our return on Sunday evening, to our dismay, we couldn't find the car – it had been stolen.

We had only had the car a few months having purchased it after I came off HMS *Phoebe*, so it was a real blow. We reported it at the Southampton Police Station and then had to figure how to get home. Between us we didn't have enough money for two train tickets back home, so we caught the train to London and had to cross London to Plaistow to visit Christine's aunt to ask her to lend us some money. We then had to go to Kings Cross and catch a train to Hull. Thankfully brother Dick came to pick us up to save us having to wait for the train to Bridlington which didn't run very frequently at that time of the night. We eventually got home gone midnight and Christine was at work early the next morning. Not a nice experience. We were later told that it was found burnt out in the New Forest somewhere. We never did hear what had happened to the perpetrators!

Chapter 4

Becoming The Royal Navy Sailing Coach

Christine and I married in June 1971, after four years together. We were married at the Priory Church in Bridlington; Chris Wright was my best man, returning the favour as I was his best man when he married Lynda a few years previously. We had a great reception at Ye Olde Star Inn which was an old coaching house situated in the 'Old Town' in Bridlington.

In those days, of course, you had your lunch and then left. However, Christine's parents had organised a party back at their house, so the celebrations went on quite a bit longer! We left for Portsmouth the next day, where I was based at the time. As our car had recently been stolen, the garage from where we bought it kindly lent us a car in which to travel down south. Of course, they expected us to buy a replacement car from them when one became available, and we bought another 1100. This we eventually returned to them as the gear box was faulty and we did without a car after that until 1973 when we bought our Vauxhall Viva Estate.

Unfortunately, at the last minute, I was drafted to Plymouth for six months in August that year to serve on HMS *Forth*, which was 'parked' in Plymouth Docks. So our plans to settle in Portsmouth were dropped but we had nowhere to live until we moved to Plymouth, so Christine returned home! However, our great friends David and Helen Swann came to the rescue and invited us to stay with them for six weeks. As I said previously, I served with Dave on HMS *Phoebe* and his lovely wife Helen was in the WRNS. We had a great time with them, they were so helpful.

Whilst we were staying with them, we put a deposit on a house that was going to be built in Gosport and would be ready for our return in January 1972. It was the middle house of three, built on a small plot of land, with two bedrooms and a carport. It cost us £6,000 and we were shocked as we could have bought a detached house in Bridlngton for the same money. However, it was a great starter home, and we had many happy times in it and quite a few great parties! We lived there for three years and then moved along the coast to Hill Head and upgraded to a semi!

Dave and Helen came out with us when we went looking for furniture and I remember one salesman asking if we were together and David telling him, "Yes we live in a commune." The look on the guy's face – he didn't know whether to believe us or not. Another amusing incident was when a tradesman came to give a price for some work they were having done and Helen said that she would have to check with her husband, but he wasn't at home. Just then I came into the room, and she said got all flustered and said, "Oh this isn't my husband!" going bright red, so Christine had to join in to spare her blushes!

Christine and I rented a flat in Mutley Plain in Plymouth. It was a three-roomed attic flat with no running hot water and the bathroom was on the floor below. The landlady could be a right battle-axe at times, but it was our first home together.

We enjoyed our stint in Plymouth: life was quite leisurely. I was still committed to sailing for the Navy and had a few weekends travelling to take part in sailing events. We enjoyed quite a few evenings in the Fortescue, a pub and restaurant in Mutley Plain. We would put our laundry in the launderette opposite and go and have a pint whilst waiting for the cycle to finish, then go back to put it in the dryer and back for another drink! Finally, our new house in Gosport was finished in February 1972 and we were very happy to move in.

On my return from Plymouth, I again went to HMS *Dryad* for around five months to gain my RP1 qualification (Radar Plotter). Whilst there, I was given the job of looking after Dryad's yacht *Planet*, which was a Van De Stadt 30 based at Hornet Sailing Centre in Gosport. *Planet* was used for sail training, crew training, skipper courses and recreational sailing.

We did some serious mileage in her, mainly in the Solent but occasionally popping across to Cherbourg to top up the wine levels! We also had some great days out sailing in the Solent with Christine's mum and dad when they came down to visit.

It was during this time when I had to call upon our maintenance team which included a certain electrician by the name of John Giblett who had never been sailing before. I took him out for a trip around the Solent and he crewed with me on a couple of the races that we entered and, after a very hairy race across to Cowes and also across to Cherbourg, he became hooked. He progressed to being a round-the-world ocean racer, competing on the Navy's Nicholson 55 *Adventure* and later skippered another Nicholson 55 *Dasher*.

When I left HMS *Dryad*, I was posted to the Royal Naval School of Seamanship, which was situated in the Flat House area in the northern end of Portsmouth Dockyard, where I was appointed as an instructor in charge of running seamanship courses, which I was really pleased about as I enjoyed teaching. I was running 12-week courses for Leading Seamen wanting to become Petty Officers. It was hard work with long hours but very rewarding.

When I arrived at the school, I was very impressed with the building which was a massive hanger and had, at one end, all the equipment required to practise anchor and towing drills as well as replenishment at sea, taking on fuel and stores. At the other end were the classrooms and all the wood was polished and varnished and ropes everywhere not unlike an old sailing vessel.

Whilst serving at the seamanship school, I had to do my

advanced leadership course at HMS *Royal Arthur* in Wiltshire, which was no holiday. We were put through our paces there, early starts and late finishes with numerous tasks thrown at us which were all to do with logistics, getting people and equipment to the right place at the right time.

The climax of the course was a trek through the Black Mountains in terrible weather conditions, with rain and fog being the main problem. We had to lead a group from 'A' to 'B' overnight and, luckily, we managed to find a barn to sleep in and dry out. We never saw the farmer who owned it, which was maybe just as well! I cannot remember how far we trekked, but it felt like around 20 miles. Since that time, I have never had the desire to go trekking in the hills again!

I was still heavily involved in sailing for the Navy, and I was appointed Captain of the Navy Dinghy Team. It was a full-on racing programme, competing in races all around the UK. We mainly did our team racing in inland waters, reservoirs and lakes but one of my favourite venues was the Inter-Services Regatta at Seaview on the Isle of Wight. We were always made very welcome by the club members.

Next came along my dream job; I was given the position of Royal Navy Sailing Coach, taking over from Roy Mullender who was famous for his offshore racing skills and skippering the Royal Navy yacht *Adventure* in the Round the World Yacht Race. During my time as Sailing Coach I managed to win the Bosun National Championships twice, once in 1975 and again in 1976 which, in those days, was not easy as there was normally a fleet of around 90 boats on the start line, with a great deal of talent. So, I was well chuffed to win that with my crew John Rothwell who I served with on the *Phoebe*.

I suppose this is when my race training seriously began as I was appointed to raise the standards of the Royal Navy teams. I focused my race training on having a development programme based on three levels. The first was the 'Introductory level' for those who had already learnt how to sail and wished to progress to racing. The second was the 'Intermediate level' for those who had completed the first level and now wanted to be more proficient in the ten aspects of the sport. Finally, the third was the 'Advanced level' for sailors who were keen to be champions at club, national or international levels of competition.

All three levels were based on a logical progression of learning, covering the various aspects of the sport:

- Self preparation
- Boat preparation
- Boat handling
- Boat tuning
- Race strategy
- Starting
- Tactics
- Racing rules
- Compass work
- Meteorology

The level of knowledge increases as the participants progress through the three course programme. All three programmes were run over a period of six days.

I ran many of these race training courses during my time as the Navy Sailing Coach as well as organising coaches' courses for both sail and race training. They were very enjoyable days and I met some good sailors during that time, many of whom went on to win championship titles in the sailing world.

In the autumn of 1972, Christine and I competed in the Portsmouth Frostbite Series in a Bosun dinghy. Christine could not swim so I was not allowed to capsize! This took place every Sunday morning in Portsmouth Harbour in all weathers until late November. There were some very talented sailors competing with very close racing. I am pleased to say we won! Second place was an Enterprise sailed by Tim Golding.

The following year I did the Fareham Sailing Club Winter Series in a Fireball with Tony Belben, which was sailed from Fareham Creek into Portsmouth Harbour and which we also managed to win. We always looked forward to our tot of rum to warm us up once we got ashore – it was freezing out there as you can well imagine.

Interlude 1: The Ten Aspects Of The Sport

1. SELF PREPARATION: If you wish to stand on the podium at any major event you must be prepared both physically and mentally. It will take a minimum of twelve weeks of fitness training to survive, especially if it is a windy event with two races a day and also to make it through the social programme! It only takes a split second to pick up an injury and become unfit, so look after yourself. Mentally you will only have the confidence to succeed when you have completed your training programme both on and off the water.

2. BOAT PREPARATION: Once you have prepared yourself, you must now prepare the boat. Gear failure at any major event is not acceptable, so daily checks need to be carried out especially after a windy day on the water. If required, make sure that you have a valid measurement certificate, take it with you and make sure that your boat is legal. Any measurement failure could mean that your boat will not be allowed on the water and all your time and effort and money will be wasted.

3. BOAT HANDLING: Tacking, gybing, spinnaker hoists and drops and mark rounding techniques across the wind range and sea state all need to be perfected during your training programme. It is all about mileage and time on the water.

4. BOAT TUNING: It takes time once again, both on and off the water, to understand what makes your racing machine go fast in a straight line on and off the wind and across the wind range and sea state. Once again this is all down to mileage.

5. RACE STRATEGY: Now that we are fit enough and have a legal boat which is going fast in a straight line, we need to know which way to point it on the racetrack. I wish that I had a pound coin for each time I have seen a ferret going very fast in the wrong direction (including myself occasionally)! Wind direction, tide and surface current, land masses, weather systems and clouds all need to be evaluated and studied. The modern racing ferrets have all done their homework before they leave the shore and know exactly which way to go both up and downwind.

6. STARTING: With a stable wind direction and strength, starting can be ninety per cent of doing well in a race. With an unstable wind direction and strength, it may be only thirty per cent of doing well. One exception could be the start of The Round the World Yacht Race! Which way you are going up the beat will determine which third of the line to start from: port, middle or starboard. To make a good start being on the front row in clear wind is a must to achieve this. The heart rate will be at its highest, unless you are gybing in twenty knots plus!

7. TACTICS: There are three areas to cover here, boat to boat, boat to group and finally boat to fleet. Tacticians must have a brain working similar to that of a chess player, focussing not only on the current surroundings, but the next move and even beyond further along the racetrack.

8. RACING RULES: Many races have been lost because of the lack of knowledge of the racing rules. In the good old days, when I won my first European gold medal crewing for Lord Nelson, there was only one racing rule, luff them and leave them! Today there are 92 rules, and you must have a good working knowledge of them if you want to be on the podium at the end of the event. You must first learn the Fundamental Rules followed by the Definitions otherwise you cannot use the rules. These should be followed by Part Two of the Racing Rules then Part Four, Part Five and Part Three. Use them as both your attacking and defensive weapons.

9. COMPASS WORK: Use of the compass is very important for your orientation of the racecourse to establish course bearings, wind shifts and the favoured end of the starting line. There will be times when you cannot see the next mark, so by knowing and following the course bearings you will eventually arrive at it. On rounding the leeward mark establish straight away whether you are on a lift or a header. In shifty conditions with an offshore wind you will want to be on the lifting tack straight away.

10. METEOROLOGY: Weather systems, clouds, cold fronts and warm fronts will affect both the wind direction and speed. The lower the cloud base, the more unstable the wind becomes, the higher it is, the more stable it will become. A good working knowledge of this subject can turn your race on its head, going from nowhere in the race to the front and hopefully onto the podium.

Chapter 5

My Olympic Campaigning

In 1970s the Olympic Sailing Committee elected to include a smaller dinghy in the next Games and the 470 was chosen. The Royal Navy decided to acquire a couple of these boats and I was given the opportunity to sail one, so I was once again on the Olympic trail. Unfortunately although Christine and I had won the Frostbite Trophy together she had no real experience at crewing and so was not Olympic material! So, having seen Tim Golding in action, I contacted him and asked him if he would be my crew. He was a very talented sailor, the right weight and height for the boat and he was also a sailmaker which would be very helpful to our campaign.

Whilst I was sailing the 470, I was drafted to HMS *Undaunted* which was undergoing refit, firstly in Portland Harbour and then Portsmouth, so it allowed me to travel to sailing events at the weekends.

Our first 470 was K131 which we based at Stokes Bay Sailing Club in Gosport where we would train in readiness for all the future events around the UK and internationally. Tim and I had some great times racing the 470 and had some successes as well as disappointments, as we all did at that level of competition, but we gained a great deal from our experiences both at home and abroad.

This new Olympic class had attracted many top racing 'ferrets' of the time and we competed against the likes of Jeremy Bickerton and Richard Butcher, Nick and Rob Martin, Nigel and

David Barrow, Phil Crebbin and Derek Clarke, Eddie Warden Owen and Ossie Stewart, Laurie Smith and Andy Barker, to name just a few. They were all top-class sailors and between us all we had some great races and learnt from each other as the campaign trail rolled on.

There was no financial assistance back then and we were all self funded (except for the fact that my boat was sponsored by the Royal Navy) and all travel and accommodation costs incurred in attending the various championships came out of your own pocket. This meant that on many occasions your accommodation was a tent with a primus stove for cooking.

One international regatta springs to mind and that was the European Championships, June 1975, held in Masnou, Spain. Tim, Christine and I had never driven in Europe before and looked at the map and picked the straightest route to our destination. We took the ferry to Le Havre and drove non-stop to the Pyrenees and over the top through the night. Talk about 'hairy', the winding road never stopped: we went up one mountain and down the other side just to see another one ahead of us. Anyway, we made it and found a good campsite and pitched our tent next to Jeremy Bickerton. It was a great regatta; and we gained a great deal of experience in competing internationally, getting some results in the top ten which was good for our first international outing.

Jeremy showed us a different way to go home which he said was much better and we finished up travelling over the mountains surrounded by snow (we thought we heard wolves howling!). We suddenly noticed that the car was pulling to one side when braking and realised that we were low on brake fluid. This meant using the brakes as little as possible, so we made our way home with Tim using the handbrake to slow us down – a very nerve-racking journey, and we were all glad when we reached the ferry port at Le Havre!

Extract from article by Dave White:

An all-too-familiar sounding story has emerged from the 470 European Championships held at Masnou, Barcelona last week. There are no prizes for guessing the identity of the nation whose two representatives suffered the indignity of having the least support of all the nations represented.

Just to give an indication as to how much we are falling behind other countries in supporting the 470 class I will detail just what this lack of support amounted to.

Firstly, we were the only country (and every major European yachting nation, with the exception of Finland, was represented) at the event without a team coach and support boat. This meant that our boys usually had to set off in the morning one hour before all the others to sail to the starting area instead of having the luxury of a tow. Also our two representatives did not get to know weather and tidal information from other parts of the course before the start, nor did they receive any other coaching benefits.

There are no prizes either for guessing which team were living it rough in tents and also had no smart uniforms for the opening and closing ceremonies. It is no coincidence surely that the top countries, at the moment, the French and Spanish, were comfortably ensconced in the best hotels, living on special diets and generally being cosseted by team managers and coaches.

In spite of all this, however, the performance of our two representatives in the eighty-boat fleet was most encouraging. Perhaps it is a pity that our boys did do so well because it will probably mean that, as a country, we will continue to attempt to run our

Olympic effort on a shoestring right through to the regatta in 1976

How things have changed! Thankfully.

Another regatta we attended was Kiel Week in Germany, again we drove there in our Vauxhall Viva but this time it was the radiator that developed a leak. In those days there was always a British Naval ship doing guard duty during the regatta and, on this occasion, luckily I had a mate on board in the engineering department, so we drove to the ship and the lads fixed the leak for us and gave us a few drinks as well!

My next 470 was K248 and we once again had some success with her. Once more we travelled abroad, and another journey of note was travelling to Hyères on the south coast of France for the Easter Regatta. To save money we travelled with our mates Peter Bateman and Patrick Lilley in Peter's Vauxhall Ventura, the 470 was on the roof of the car and Peter's Flying Dutchman on a trailer. All was going splendidly and we were on the motorway near Lyon, playing cards to pass the time (Pat steering with his knee so he could hold his cards), when there was an almighty bang; cards and money went everywhere and the prop shaft dropped out of the bottom of the car!

Luckily we managed to make a phone call to Peter's boss at Bruce Banks Sails and they very kindly organised a new prop shaft and took it to Heathrow to be flown out to us. We were stuck at the side of the road with the boats laid out on the verge for 36 hours waiting for this replacement to arrive at Lyon Airport. The weather was freezing cold and we had to wear most of our clothes and wrap towels around our heads in order to keep warm. Anyway, we fixed it and made the regatta on time, an experience that we could have done without!!

We continued to travel to most of the foreign regattas by car. As you can see, they were not always reliable ones, so, if we could, we would travel in convoy, just in case we had a car or trailer issue. On one occasion on a trip to the south of France four of us, towing our 470s, arrived in Paris at the large roundabout which circles the Arc de Triomphe at the top end of the Champs-Élysées and we had no idea which exit we should take. Having circumnavigated it once in convoy we decided to stop and ask the Gendarme in control which exit we should take. So he halted all the traffic to allow us to safely leave the roundabout at the right exit. He was not amused!

I think that this was also the journey when, whilst returning home, we were following Jeremy Bickerton when we noticed that his trailer had ripped off the back end of his car, a well-used Volkswagen Beetle. We managed to fix it by tying a rope to his trailer and lashing it over the roof of the car onto the front bumper. This made the rest of trip home quite entertaining for him! When he returned home he was able to get a new back end re-welded ready for the next trip. Another 'hairy journey'!

After three years of solid training, touring around the UK and Europe to compete in events we obtained our third and final boat, K351, for the Olympic trials in Weymouth in June 1976. We were on a high having won the final indicator trial at Hayling Island the previous weekend. As you would expect, it was a hotly contested series as all helmsmen and crews were by now experienced at racing the 470.

Throughout the week the weather was a mixed bag, including force six south-westerly gusty conditions and light shifty breezes. Our results included two seconds, a third, a fourth and a sixth. Phil Crebbin and Derek Clarke won, and we finished sixth having suffered a broken rudder blade during a windy race whilst lying third at the time. 'BOAT PREPARATION'! We had to count the retirement as we also had an OCS earlier in the week – a case of 'if only'! We were trying too hard but as the famous Dane, Paul Elvstrom, said to me "If you don't have an OCS on your score sheet, you are not trying hard enough."

Dave White had rented a flat on the sea front for the week and decided to organise a class party at the end of the trials which, with hindsight, he probably wished he hadn't! What a night that was, as guests arrived at the front door, they received a bucket of water from the balcony above ensuring that everyone was soaked to the skin when they entered. When we arrived we saw all the water on the pavement and realised what was happening so rang the door bell and immediately jumped out of the way and avoided the deluge!

What a great party that was! The flat was in such a mess that the following day some of us had to go back and assist Dave to clean up before he could return it to the owners and get his deposit back! Thanks, Dave, for a great 'do', it rounded off the three year campaign perfectly as a good time was had by all.

After the Olympic trials I continued my post as the Royal Navy Sailing Coach and I was asked to organise a Royal Navy sailing coach's course, which would be assessed and examined by the RYA National Sailing Coach / Examiner, Bob Bond. The course was to be set up and run at HMS *Excellent*'s brand new sailing centre on Whale Island in Portsmouth. Preparation for the five day course was intense as I had to ensure that the coaches I selected to attend the course were some of our best and that all the requirements to run the course were in place before Bob Bond arrived on Monday morning.

Bob and I got on very well together and the course was a success. At the end of the five days Bob informed me that he had been very impressed with the course and I was happy that the majority of the candidates passed with flying colours. Little did I know at the time what an important part this meeting with Bob would play in my future life.

During my time as the Royal Navy Sailing Coach I also operated from HMS *Temeraire* which was the Royal Navy School of Physical Training and it was from there that I ran the fitness training sessions for the Royal Navy Sailing Team. When I became the RYA Racing Coach the Navy kindly allowed me to take members of the Olympic, Womens' and Youth Squads to *Temeraire* and also HMS *Excellent* once a week for training which worked really well and was good public relations for both the Navy and the RYA.

I had done so much sailing all over the UK and Europe that I just wanted to take time out from the sport, it was burn out time! My time as the Royal Navy Sailing Coach was coming to an end and reality was about to kick in! It was time to go back to sea.

I had been promoted as Chief Petty Officer Operations Radar; in charge of the Operations Room onboard HMS *Hermione*. I have to say this turned out to be the worst ship that I had ever served on. The ship was bad from the captain downwards and it never really worked. We failed our sea trials badly and morale was at an all time low, so much so that I was called upon by the Flag Officer Sea Training Portland Admiral Pritchard, whom I served with on the *Phoebe*, to give my opinion as to why things were not going as well as they should be. Admiral Pritchard was a great officer, in my opinion, hard but fair, I had a great deal of respect for him as did many other Royal Naval personnel. The Captain of the *Hermione* was replaced, we went through sea trials again and this time we passed. On completion of our trials, we joined the fleet and were soon to be part of a NATO squadron working with the US Sixth Fleet in the Mediterranean Sea.

It was whilst I was serving on HMS *Hermione* in 1977 that I was invited by the RYA to attend their Head Office in Woking for an interview for a new position as the National Yacht Racing Coach which I did at my earliest opportunity. I didn't find out until later that there were 144 applicants for the job.

I thought that the interview had gone badly, and I returned to the *Hermione* which was in Portsmouth at the time. I never gave it much thought afterwards as I was sure that I wouldn't get the job. We sailed back to the Mediterranean after a short spell back in the UK to rejoin the US Sixth Fleet.

It was during this time that I received a telegram from the

59

RYA saying that I had got the job, subject to my leaving the Navy within six months. What a shock to the system that was, as it was so unexpected! I didn't hold out much hope of being released from the Royal Navy within six months as in those days you had to give 18 months notice to leave the Navy. However, here was that perfect scenario of: it is not always what you know, but who you know!

It just happened that John Durie, the Secretary General of the Royal Yachting Association, knew the Commander in Chief of Portsmouth who was also the Commodore of the Royal Naval Sailing Association and who I knew personally from all my naval sailing days. So they talked to each other and in no time at all I was leaving HMS *Hermione*, whilst at anchor in the Solent for the Spithead review to celebrate the Queen's Silver Jubilee 1977.

Christine picked me up at the Gosport ferry and asked me where my shoes were, as I was in my stocking feet. I had no idea where I had lost them as the lads had given me a good send off! I attended HMS Nelson barracks in Portsmouth the following Monday to be discharged from the service and I shall never forget what the Master at Arms said to me as I was about to leave. He told me that the only other person he knew who had legally left the Royal Navy as quickly as me was Prince Phillip when his wife became the Queen!

After 15 great years in the Royal Navy I was out. I am forever grateful for my life in the Royal Navy, it was great for character building. I made some lifelong friends with whom I remain in contact with after all those years: Stuart Lawson, Dave Swann, Pete and Joyce Bowler, John Giblett, Brian Dunn, to name but a few.

Interlude 2: Sailing International Regattas

Fortunately, so much has changed for British sailors competing on the international circuit – often the boats will be taken for them, and they won't be in a tent with a primus! But much of what I learnt over that period in the 1970s is still just as relevant today and that is 'forward planning'.

Make sure that all your travel arrangements are made in good time and that all your paperwork is up to date, especially your passport! Organise good accommodation so that you sleep well. Allow yourself enough time to prepare for measurement (if required), to check racecourse orientation and conditions – i.e. sea state and the wind.

Having a coach to support you both on and off the water is important, especially to tow you to and from the race area, more so in light winds, which can save so much of your time.

Establish a daily routine – i.e. times to get out of your basket, have breakfast, go down to the boat park, leave the marina, arrive in the race area, have a debrief, evening meal, get back into your basket and have a good sleep.

Make sure that you have a nutritional and rehydration programme in place, carbohydrates to take in between races and within an hour after racing. Ensure you have sufficient energy drinks – you need to drink more than you think; if you feel you are losing your concentration it is a sure sign that you are becoming dehydrated.

Sorting out all the above prior to the event will give you more confidence to do well and finish in a podium position.

Chapter 6

Setting Up The RYA Youth Programme

I joined the Royal Yachting Association at their office in Woking
three days after my thirtieth birthday − what a life changing
experience that was. As the new RYA National Yacht Racing
Coach, I was introduced to the rest of the team in the office −
there were eleven of us in total (there would be 86 in the office
when I left in 2000 after the Sydney Olympics). My boss was
Bob Bond, the RYA National Sailing Coach / Training Manager
but my real boss was my secretary, Sally Carmichael; she was
brilliant. She kept me in line for the 11 years we worked in
Woking, although I was hardly ever there and only popped in
at the end of each month to sort out my expenses! Sally was a
great organiser and managed both myself and Bob − how she
put up with us both I don't know, she deserved a medal the size
of a frying pan!

The RYA told me to go out and find a car suitable for the job
of carrying bodies, equipment and towing. I acquired a Ford
Cortina two-litre estate car, which was perfect for the job as I was
able to fit a roof rack capable of carrying a dinghy.

The next item to acquire was a coach boat. John Reed, the
RYA Racing Manager, was a good friend of Norman Fletcher,
the owner of Fletcher Boats, who generously supplied us with a
Fletcher sports boat free of charge. This was an ideal boat with
plenty of space for carrying bodies and equipment and during
my time at the RYA I was given four of these boats and the great
thing about them was that I never needed to pump or patch

them up!

The Royal Yachting Association had employed me to raise the standards of yacht / dinghy racing within the United Kingdom. In 1977 Bob Bond, Alistair Mitchell (Scottish Coach) and the RYA Council had recognised that if we, as a nation, did not ramp up our racing standards we would not be performing on the international stage in the future and they were absolutely correct in their thinking. I had already been giving this serious thought before I arrived and had come to the conclusion that the only way forward was to work with the youth of today to prepare them for tomorrow and beyond.

I put my proposals together, which was to establish a National Youth Racing Scheme based at club, regional and national level. There were to be three levels of race training based on a badge scheme:

- The **RED** badge was the Introductory Level for those who had completed a sail training programme
- The **WHITE** badge was for Intermediate Level for those who had completed the previous course
- The **BLUE** badge was the Advanced level for those who had completed the previous two courses

On completion of each stage, the ferrets were very keen to stitch their badges onto their buoyancy aids to display them. The sailing clubs would have to sign up to this and we would then put in place Club Racing Instructor courses.

The plan was submitted to the RYA Training Committee at the time and they approved it and agreed the funding for it on the proviso that we had five years in which to prove the system and show results after which the programme would be judged as either a success or a failure and, if it were the latter, it would be scrapped.

The rest, as they say, is history! I spent the next 23 years averaging 40,000 miles per annum in a car travelling around the United Kingdom and Europe and flying further afield (New Zealand 16 times!!), attending international training and events. It was to be a fabulous time working with the best of British sailors from a very early age.

A hot political potato at the time was that the whole youth programme was going to be based around a small number of youth classes who would receive RYA funding and coaching support. Those classes were to be Optimist, Topper, Mirror, Cadet, Europe, Laser and 420. This decision upset those who were not included, but these were the top international youth classes at that time, which would ultimately feed the Olympic programme. These classes would be reviewed every five years and decisions made as to whether or not they would remain in the programme or be changed depending on world developments.

The programme really kicked off with a pilot scheme which was run by both me and Eric Twiname at Queen Mary Sailing Club over a five-day period in the summer holidays. Queen Mary Sailing Club was really the birthplace of the GBR Race Training Scheme. It was from there that we went for the official launch in the summer of 1977.

In order to get the Race Training Programme 'out there' we invited interested clubs to come along to a presentation about the whole scheme at the London Boat Show. We were pleased to see that many did attend, sending their representatives along to hear all about it. The clubs became more and more involved as the years went by which was great to see, as without them supporting the whole programme it was never going to get off the ground.

In my first year at the RYA, John Barker, who was the Youth Team Manager and a member of the RYA Training Committee, and myself went to the International Yacht Racing Union (IYRU, now World Sailing) World Youth Championships, as it was called in those days, in France, where the GBR team did badly, finishing in the bottom third of the fleet in both classes.

I was born into sailing: my model of the yacht Mona owned by John and Les Rix, with whom I would crew for later in their Dragon class yacht Monatoo. The model was built by my father.

Here we are, the three musketeers, hooligans in the making. Mum went grey at a young age putting up with us three!!

Me in my newly painted little red car! I got my passion for cars at a young age!

Practising our sculling in Bridlington Harbour with cousin Robin.

My first command in the Royal Navy in a 32-foot sailing cutter on the River Stour, HMS Ganges, 1963.

Helming a Navy cutter at HMS Ganges.

In my Number One suit having just been presented with my first-class coxswain's award at the age of sixteen at HMS Ganges, 1963.

On board HMS Delight, 1964/1965. This was a two-and-a-half-year commission with a cruise to the Far East. She was a great ship, a proper destroyer.

Rounding Cape of Good Hope on our way to Cape Town on board HMS Phoebe, 1970. There were moments when we thought that we would become submariners!

Crewing for Alex Macleod on his Dragon Bonaventure at the Edinburgh Cup in Poole. As a director of Grants Whisky, he always had a good supply of 'the wee dram' in the boot of his Ferrari!

21ˢᵗ birthday celebrations at the Haven Hotel in Sandbanks.

The Big Day: Christine and I married on 26 June, 1971 at the Priory Church in Bridlington.

The Royal Navy dinghy team having just won the Inter-Services Championships — more celebrations!

Bosun National Champions with John Rothwell 1976 in a fleet of 90 boats.

Sailing the 470 with Tim Golding when we won the final indicator trial at Hayling Island in 1976, the week before the Olympic trials.

The first Royal Navy coaches' course at HMS Excellent observed and assessed by Bob Bond on my starboard side.

Mimi Currey and Jill Blake receiving coaching from me at the Women's Worlds in Rochester, 1979.

The two Jim Saltonstalls when we met in 1980 in Rhode Island, USA.

A very proud moment, having won the Yachtsman of the Year Award with the UK Youth Team, 1984: Jason Belben, Andy Hemmings, myself and Stuart Childerley.

Steering the 12-metre White Crusader in 1986 during trials / training for the America's Cup off Freemantle, Australia.

Escorting Princess Anne to the RYA flagship during the UK Youth Championships at Lake Bala.

The pinnacle of our successes at the World Youth Championship, winning the Nautica Nations Cup for the best national team at the 1995 championship in Bermuda.

On board Luder during the J24 National Championships at Poole with Eddy Owen, Brian Hodge, Adrian Friend, Ossie Stewart where we won the gold medal.

Meeting 'Betty' at Buckingham Palace and being presented with the MBE in 1997 – the highlight of my coaching career.

All smiles with Ben Ainslie after winning his gold medal in Sydney 2000.

Some of our successful Olympians at the medal ceremony on the Sydney Opera House steps.

John Cook's yacht Cristabella. Five years as their supporter – an awesome team of professional sailors achieving some good results in the early days of the TP52 circuit.

The Dragon World Champions in 2013: Jamie Lee, Klaus Deitrich, me (coach) and Andy Beadsworth.

John and I looked at each other and said, "Never again." We went back to the UK and began setting up the different courses at club, regional and national levels during the school holidays and weekends throughout the year including the winter months. These courses culminated in the National Youth Championships and Selection Trials being held over the Easter holidays to pick the youth team which would represent GBR at the World Youth Championships later in the year. If the World Championships were in the southern hemisphere, during our winter, we had the trials during the autumn.

John Barker was, at that time, a captain in the Royal Navy whom I knew from my Navy sailing days. He was a great man who put his heart and soul into the whole programme and carried out his work in committee with determination, making sure that we had everything that we needed to make the whole scheme a success. He was very much a part of the success of GBR yachting that we have today. Amongst the early participants in our Youth Programme were sailors who have gone on to bigger things in their careers and whose names are widely recognised today in yachting circles.

Winter training was an important part of preparing the ferrets for this major competition, which was held each year at a different club within England, Scotland and Wales. A young lad asked me why I called them 'ferrets', to which I replied, because like a ferret you are very intelligent and very fast like 'ferrets up a drainpipe' and it grew from there.

Rutland, Grafham and Queen Mary Sailing Clubs played a major role in its success over 23 years 1977-2000. We had nothing but praise for what those clubs did for the RYA Youth Programme, and I am pleased to see that it still happens to this very day.

During the night I would be patrolling the accommodation areas to make sure that all the ferrets were asleep in their correct 'baskets'! There were times when it was very tough for the ferrets, physical training was compulsory at 0700 Saturday and Sunday mornings, which was not very popular. I would drag them all out of their 'baskets' kicking and screaming, and we would go jogging and do various exercises before breakfast. I would shout at them, "I don't want to see tears of pain, I want to see tears of gratitude, only the fittest will win!"

Winter training started in January and on some occasions it was so cold that the reservoirs would be frozen and we would have to break the ice on the shoreline in order to get the boats in the water. The main, jib and spinnaker sheets would be frozen solid, and the ferrets would have to take them into the showers to thaw them out! I will say this, not many of them complained because they were so keen to get going.

Extract from Bob Fisher 'Airs his view' in Yachts & Yachting:
For National Racing Coach read Martinet. I've seen some slave drivers in my time, but Sunny Jim Saltonstall takes the all-time lead. For all the right reasons, of course. If you think that the race training courses for youth is nothing more than an excuse for the kids to have a good time then you should take the time to see Jim in action at Queen Mary as I did the other day. Certainly no rest cure, but there can be no doubt that it is beginning to pay dividends already.

It was after one of the training weekends when I learnt something about towing a boat. One of the ferrets asked me if I could tow his 420 back to the south coast for him from Grafham Water. Being a friendly coach from the county of Yorkshire, I said "Yes, no problem, hook it onto the back of the 'Swedish hearse'." On my journey south I was driving the car by steering with my knee whilst pouring out a cup of Yorkshire Tea from my Thermos. I looked in my rear-view mirror and saw that the 420 on its trailer had come unhooked from the car and was following me in a straight line down the A1M at approximately 50 miles per hour! I threw my cup into the passenger well, grabbed the steering wheel with both hands and saw all the traffic astern had either pulled up or slowed down, waiting for the worst to happen. As the trailer was following me I thought, 'do I let it crash into the back of me or just slow down as it was until it stops.' We got down to approximately ten miles per hour when it veered into the outside lane and stopped; I jumped out, hooked it back on and drove off!

The moral of the story is always personally hook a boat onto your car towing ball as obviously, on this occasion, the ferret had not fastened it on correctly. That was a very lucky escape as no damage had been caused thanks to the jockey wheel on the trailer being locked off at the right height in the fore and aft position.

The other consideration, taken in the early stages, was to get involved with the National Schools Sailing Association which was doing great work training young sailors in the schools. The RYA always wanted to have a good working relationship with them as they saw them as one of the main feeders of good talent into the National Youth Squad. To this end, I would attend the NSSA National Championships to have an input and identify talent to progress into the GBR Youth Squad. This relationship has continued ever since and many of our top ferrets originated from the good work of the NSSA.

And so the GBR Race Training Scheme unfurled. It became so successful with the youth programme that the adults also wanted to be involved. So we extended the programme by running more club racing coach training courses and club racing seminars for their members. Class associations also wanted more race training, so they established specific race training coaches for their class and so the scheme grew bigger and bigger over the years.

During the very early stages of developing the Youth Programme in 1978, both Bob Bond and John Reed, agreed that it would be a good idea to find a sponsor for the UK Youth Team and support them by providing a team kit both on and off the water when representing the UK at the World Youth Championships. Mr Henri Strezlecki, the co founder and owner of Henri Lloyd Ltd, agreed to meet me at their head office in Manchester and immediately agreed to be a sponsor. This began an incredible partnership with the Youth Programme which lasted for the whole of my tenure at the RYA. Henri and his family also became very close personal friends of ours. We could not thank Henri Lloyd enough for all their help and support during that time frame. Their financial contribution in terms of kitting out the youth team was awesome; our teams always looked the part both on and off the water. Many thanks Mr Henri, we will never forget what both you and your company did for British Youth Sailing over many years.

Whist talking about youth sponsorship, during the early 1990s there was a new development in match racing, so we decided to develop a National Youth Match Racing Programme which, like the fleet racing, quickly took off and became very popular in producing our top match racers for the future. I couldn't possibly have asked Henri Lloyd to also sponsor this programme, so I went to see Keith Musto who very kindly took on the support of our new venture. So we were very grateful to the Musto Company for their support. Over the years we also received sponsorship from other sources, Crewsavers, Javelin and Tilbury Docks to name only a few. All of them played a part in the successes we achieved in the youth training that made our great sailors of today.

Interlude 3: Running A Youth Training Programme

Working with young racing ferrets can be very rewarding and they must be kept busy at all times otherwise they soon become bored – not good for morale! So, as well as the morning keep fit exercises, we gave them on the water exercises after which we carried out video debriefs analysing and evaluating everything to help them improve their performance the next time they went on the water.

Most importantly, they should be enjoying their sailing over and above their performance as, if you get this wrong, they will lose interest and leave sailing.

When working with young racing ferrets we need to be careful about the number of days they spend training and attending events each year because if they do too many they can easily become 'burnt out' which we want to avoid. There are other activities that they will want to do with friends and family and these need to be included in order to get the correct balance in their lives as they are physically and mentally developing.

They must also take into consideration their education as some ferrets can become so committed to their sailing that they forget about this. As their coach you may occasionally need to remind them that their education comes first. They can be successful in both as we have seen in the past on numerous occasions. I recall taking a youth team to New Zealand on one occasion when they did their homework at 35,000 feet on both the outbound and inbound legs of their journey. They won the gold medal and passed their exams, so it can be done.

Chapter 7

Moving On To The International Stage

From the beginning the RYA also had a National Women's Squad and their training programme was run parallel with the youth programme which worked very well as both groups learnt from each other and created good competition. The women had already had successes at the IYRU Women's World Championships. The women's team sailed hard and played hard, we had some memorable events over the years. In Holland one year we had a party on the night before the last race, Cathy Foster and Wendy Hilder were having a great championship and they only needed to finish in 14th place or above to secure the gold medal. When they came round the first mark they were lying 14th and looked a little under the weather! However, they pulled it off and we won the gold!

Another championship of note was in Rochester, New York State on Lake Ontario, where Cathy and Wendy again took gold in the 420 class. The party was amazing, and it culminated with people being thrown into the showers. The problem was that the showers were on the same level as the lounge which was carpeted and soaked up the water which then met with the wallpaper. When we returned the next day the club was in a terrible mess. I visited again a couple of years later after the Youth Worlds in Texas and the club had been completely redecorated. The Commodore told me that it was the best party in the club's history!

Over the years we have had some amazing prize-givings,

especially when we were on the podium. At the Women's Worlds in Scotland, the social scene was awesome and with the medals came the prize-giving which went on until daylight – a good time had by all. Another Women's' World Championship I recall was in La Rochelle where again Cathy Foster and Wendy Hilder won the gold medal and the other members of the team were stood on a thick marble table jumping up and down, cheering and singing when the marble top suddenly broke in half. All I could do was put each half under my arms and go to the bar and apologise and offer to pay for it. Thankfully I was told not to worry, that it happened all the time and was part of the fun! I was lucky to get away with that one as I would have had to part with quite a few French francs!

On another occasion at a pre-Olympic regatta in Barcelona a few of us piled into a taxi to go to the prize-giving when two young ladies asked if they could have a lift with us. I shouted "Jump in love and sit on my knee" also adding a cheeky comment. A horrified voice said, "You can't say that Jim, she's Princess Cristina, the King of Spain's daughter!" Well I didn't know!

The success of the women's team rubbed off onto the youth squad and soon the top youth sailors at the time were also starting to make a name for themselves at both national and international level which was most encouraging as they had started to move up the rankings at the IYRU World Youth Championships.

We attended the IYRU World Youth Championships 1978 in Perth, Australia and 1979 in Livorno, Italy but our first success came in 1980 at Fort Worth, Texas when the GBR team included Ricky Tagg and Ian Jarrett sailing the Laser Two and Andrew Brown sailing the Laser One. Ricky and Ian finished fourth and Andrew took the silver medal. A great result for our youth ferrets and a sign that the system at home was beginning to produce sailors capable of being at the top of the international stage.

The hospitality at Fort Worth was amazing. Club members loaned each nation's competitors their houses, which were all on the lake site set in a large, landscaped area, with fridges full of ferret fodder and drink. The family who loaned us their house took us out for a meal and we had a steak which was the size of our Sunday roast!! We were taken into Fort Worth for a day out and then in the evening we were taken to The Grand Ole Opry. The journey home was quite something: we travelled in a yellow school bus and, unbeknown to us, the driver had been drinking and was behaving slightly erratically! Suddenly we heard police sirens and we were pulled over and we all had to get off the bus and continue our way on foot. Thankfully we were almost back at our digs! We heard later that the Commodore of the sailing club had managed to smooth things over; I think he was the local Mayor!

There was a golf buggy with our accommodation to get around the site and one day we decided to use it to go to the shops. The only problem was that it was uphill and we had to get out and push it to give it a helping hand. Coming back was OK. A police car came by and slowed down, so we all waved at them and they took one look and just drove on!

The prize-giving was a very sociable affair, the club members all attended, and they were all very smartly turned out. All the teams joined in together and Dave Perry, the USA coach, played the piano and we had a great singsong. As the night got into full flow quite a few people ended up in the swimming pool fully clothed including the ladies of the club in all their finery and jewellery, but everyone had a great evening, one to remember. The next morning the pool was covered in a layer of oily make-up!

After the event, with the ferrets on their way back to England, I had booked some time off so that Christine and I could go up to meet the Saltonstall family (USA), and also to watch the America's Cup in Newport, Rhode Island. We had been in touch with the American 'Salties' prior to leaving the UK as I had met up with a member of their family back in 1977 in Naples,

Italy whilst I was serving on HMS *Hermione*. It was one of those surreal moments when I introduced myself to an officer in the US Navy and he was amazed that my surname was the same as his wife Susie's. She was in Italy with him and so I met up with her and we made an instant connection, our facial features were very similar.

They were most insistent that if we were in the USA we should go and visit them in Rhode Island, so that's what we did. Their branch of the family originated from the time of the Pilgrim Fathers when Sir Richard Saltonstall sailed to America on the *Arabella* and became the founder of New England. On the foreshore in Boston there is a plaque to mark where Sir Richard landed and founded the state. There is also an office block in Boston called the Saltonstall Building, after Leverett Saltonstall, who was the senator for Boston, Massachusetts. We had a great time with them.

The most astonishing moment was when I met the other Jim Saltonstall. It was quite eerie when we met: as he walked into the room it was like looking at my twin brother. He is two years older than me and he and most of the family are keen sailors. After a great holiday, as always, time to get back to the UK and onwards and upwards with the training programmes.

As the Youth Programme developed, we wanted to expose the ferrets to more international regattas to get the feel for the major events at a younger age. We felt that the experience of racing in a big fleet was very important for race strategy, tactics (especially on the starting line), the racing rules and protest procedures. All the youth classes were supported with a class coach and encouraged to go to as many international regattas as possible within their budgets.

The Optimist class in particular needed to give their ferrets the experience as this would benefit their future as they progressed through the Youth Programme and onto the World Youth Championships and possibly the Olympic Games. With this in mind we decided to send those ferrets at the senior end of the Youth Programme, in both the 420 and Laser classes, to Kiel Week which is the largest regatta in the world. We did sixteen Kiel Weeks in a row using the week as a training week: results were not a priority; it was all about the learning curve and being involved in a major event.

As a squad we stayed at the British Kiel Yacht Club army barracks which were close to the Olympic Marina. The days were long, starting at 0700 with a light fitness routine to connect the brain to the body, followed by breakfast then on to the boat park ready for the day's racing. On completion of the racing programme, it was then back to the barracks for the video debriefs and lessons to be learnt from their experience.

There were occasions when I would take some of the ferrets out to watch a race. It is amazing how much can be learnt by watching a race on the international stage. After a tough week of training both ashore and afloat, we would pack up the boats and head off back to Hamburg and the ferry to Harwich. The ferry would leave the following day and so as a treat for all their hard work we would meet up with an old school friend of mine, Geoff Garrett, who was living in Hamburg, and he would give the ferrets a guided tour of the night life and especially the Hamburg Fish Market, which opened at four o'clock in the morning and sold anything and everything under the sun. It was amazing what some ferrets would buy to take home on the ferry: a tall plant sticking through the car sunroof springs to mind!

Another incident was a bit more serious! Kiel Week was well known for the number of large national flags which flew from flag poles around the marinas, and it was well known that quite a few of them went missing as the week progressed. As always, at the beginning of the event I used to advise the ferrets not to try to acquire one, but sure enough there is always one – no names mentioned – who decided to climb a pole and grab himself a flag. However, when he appeared at the bottom of the pole he was met by 'Mr Plod' and a visit to the local 'Nick' and a hefty fine followed. You just can't tell some people!

But on the whole, it was a great experience both on and off the water for the ferrets helping to put them on the podium at many future international events at European, World and Olympic level. A good investment by the RYA for the future success of the UK in the most challenging sport in the world; more challenging than climbing Mount Everest. Why? Because there are far more variables to achieve the ultimate aim than there are in any other sport.

The Olympic classes also used Kiel Week as a training regatta and on one occasion I had the honour of supporting my old mate Eddy Warden Owen who was preparing for the Moscow Olympics in the 470 class. Ed is a brilliant sailor who shares my philosophy of work hard, play hard which is good and can often produce medals! It just so happened that Ed's birthday falls during Kiel Week which could be, and normally was, very dangerous for the liver!

As the week progressed, Ed and his crew Mark (Bones) Simpson were not doing very well, with below par results, so as his birthday was imminent, I arranged with a good sailing friend of mine, who was serving on board the guardship HMS *Glamorgan*, an invitation to an early evening cocktail party to celebrate. Ed was well impressed, he being a Welshman going on board HMS *Glamorgan* was quite special. I organised with the rest of the squad to meet up with us in a nearby large beer keller to celebrate with him, knowing that this could turn out to be a big session, and so it was! At approximately seven o'clock Edward staggered down the gangway off the ship and I recall him saying to me "That was great James, take me home, it's bedtime," to which I replied, "Sorry Edward, we cannot do that yet, there are some more of your mates waiting to have a beer with you."

We entered the bar to a raucous rendition of Happy Birthday from the whole of the British Sailing Team and sat down at the table opposite each other with a stein glass of beer with a pile of froth on the top. I blew the froth off mine, and it hit Ed full in his face, I knew what was going to happen next and sure enough he threw his beer at me. I moved sideways and it hit Debbie Gorrod full in the face. She stood up with a shocked look on her face and thumped him and down he went out for the count! I helped him to the car to take him to the barracks. As I was driving a brand new car, the lads wanted to tie him onto the roof rack with his head over the tailgate with the windscreen wiper going in case he vomited! However, I thought better of it so piled him into the back of the car and got him to his bed.

The following morning, being a Welshman, Edward had a hangover. Mark, his crew, was not impressed at all as he had to rig the boat single handed. Ed would not sail out to the race area as it was a long way, so Mark steered whilst Ed stayed in the coach boat and I towed them out at speed. Eventually we arrived in the starting area and, with a lot of encouragement, we got him into the 470 feeling decidedly 'under the weather'. It was one of those days with light shifty winds and, as you may recall, the Race Committee signalled using star shells which were very loud. Ed could not stand the noise so made his way to the port end of the line as far away from the Committee Boat as possible. He was there by himself as it was a starboard end favoured line with the fleet wanting to go right and after many general recalls Ed and Mark were still at the port end by themselves. The race started, the wind shifted to the left, Ed tacked and crossed the fleet on port tack and finished third in the race which was his best result of the week! Brilliant, it's amazing how a relaxed brain can bring out the best results after a tense start to the week!

Interlude 4: Coaching At Events

Coaching at racing events, whether at home or abroad, presents various challenges. First and foremost is how you can best support your ferrets. Don't forget that you will be their leader and with that in mind I would recommend the following actions:

- **Aims** – Identify them and how they can be achieved. Also be aware of any restrictions (if any) which may occur that could prevent you from being successful.
- **Plan** – Establish priorities
- **Brief** – Confirm understandings
- **Execute** – Maintain standards, progress, tasks
- **Evaluate** – Assess, review
- **Advise** – Listen and enthuse

You must:

- Have **Knowledge** of all aspects of racing
- Be a good **Communicator** which means engaging brain before mouth
- Have the ability to **Motivate** your ferrets to do their best
- Be a **Disciplinarian** and make sure that they are in the right place at the right time
- Be a **Manager** to manage their whole programme
- Be a **Scientist** able to create new ideas
- And above all else, be a **Friend**, possibly for life as you will not forget them, and they will not forget you

Before embarking on any event, I would recommend writing a checklist to ensure that nothing is forgotten.

Having completed a training programme, both coach and competitors can be confident that they can do well, although I always maintain that you should not enter a competition expecting to win every race as that can be when mistakes begin to creep in because you are feeling over-confident. Instead, target being consistently in the top ten in every race as it is amazing how many events are won by someone who never wins a race. Consistency is what can put you on the podium at the end.

Travel, food and accommodation are key elements to a successful event. Do not arrive too early or too late. Eat well, arrange good accommodation not too far from the venue and in a quiet area so that you can get the amount of sleep that you require: some ferrets require eight hours sleep, some need only three.

All the above played a major role to our success at the Sydney 2000 Olympic Games. Jet lag is an issue: allow four days to recover and a good night's sleep before the first race is recommended. Driving long distances is not good for a racing ferret as long-distance driving is very taxing, so this is where family and friends can really help out if they can tow the boats and allow the team members to fly out to the venue.

Before going to any major event don't forget the five 'P's: Perfect Planning Produces Perfect Performance and the four 'C's:

- **Commitment** – to the campaign
- **Concentration** – always one hundred percent
- **Confidence** – you CAN do well
- **Control** – of your emotions

Chapter 8

Youth Results Start Coming

We moved again in 1978 to a bungalow in Warsash, Christine had started working at Moody's Boatyard and Marina on the River Hamble, so it was easier for her to travel to work. Then in 1981 my personal life changed again when I became a dad. We were not really ready for this event, when Christine went into labour, she was just putting up the last pieces of wallpaper in what was going to be the nursery. By midnight on 10 December, we realised we couldn't put it off any longer and I drove her to the Princess Anne Hospital in Southampton in thick fog. Our little ferret, Jeremy, arrived at 0730 on 11 December, just in time for Christmas. Neither of us appreciated what a difference a baby would make to our lives. As with any family, when your first ferret arrives it is a life-changing experience to say the least, like walking into a brick wall!

When I was given a company car, Christine was driving a Triumph GT6 which was a fantastic little car, and we had some great drives in it. When Jeremy came along, we attached a pram seat into the well behind the two front seats so we could strap him into it for local trips. This was legal in those days! He would sit there watching everything that went on, he loved it sat between us in the back. We managed to keep this beloved Triumph GT6 for a further six years until the ferret could no longer fit into the seat between us! No wonder he picked up his driving skills very quickly and could not wait to become old enough to start motoring. When his time came, he was quickly into his Honda

Civic Type R and his Subaru Impretza, now driving a VW Golf R, another pocket rocket ship!!

In the meantime, back at HQ, all was going to plan, the youth programme was still expanding, the National Youth Squad were doing well both nationally and internationally. In 1981 and 1982 the World Youth Championships were held respectively in Sines, Portugal and Lake Como, Italy, and we finished in the top ten in both classes in both years.

Our great breakthrough came in 1983 when they were held in Auckland, New Zealand. Jason Belben and Andy Hemmings won the gold medal in the two-handed 470 class and Stuart Childerley came fourth in the Laser. This could not have come at a better time, given that my brief was to achieve success within five years and therefore the decision was made to carry on with the Youth Race Training Scheme. These results culminated in the Yachting Journalist Association awarding me and the Youth Team the prestigious Yachtsman of the Year Award so along with Jason, Andy and Stuart we went up to the London Boat Show in January 1984 to be presented with the trophy. A very proud moment.

Extract by Strahan Soames in Yachts and Yachting:
Even yachting journalists have moments when they feel that their readers must peer over the tops of their spectacles and grudgingly say: 'Well done.' Yet one such moment of glory, even of truth, was when the combined wisdom of the yachting journalists gave what is now properly but unhandily called The Yachting Journalists' Association / Domecq Yachtsman of the Year Award to the RYA's National Racing Coach, who is Jim Saltonstall, and to three startlingly successful members of his Youth Training Scheme who are Jason Belben, Andrew Hemmings and Stuart Childerley. It is also significant that a

runner-up for this award was Cathy Foster, for she was also coached by Jim Saltonstall.

The Women's Squad were still doing very well 'hoovering up' medals all over the world and the Olympic squad was also progressing well preparing for the Games in Los Angeles in 1984. The IYRU organised the Youth World Championships to be held in San Diego after the Games which gave young sailors, from all over the world, the opportunity to watch the sailing at the Games giving them the motivation to represent their countries in the future. This worked very well as the majority of them did exactly that. Stuart won the gold medal in the Laser One class and Jeremy Robinson and Paul Hooker finished fourth in the double hander. Stuart Childerley received his medal from Dennis Connor, a great honour. Little did Dennis know then that in 2002 Stuart was going to beat him at the Etchell World Championships in England and take the gold medal.

Christine and Jeremy made the trip to California with us and we were accommodated in the houses of yacht club members and made very welcome and shown wonderful hospitality. When we had some time to sightsee, we visited the *Queen Mary* and the *Spruce Goose* and we have a picture of Jeremy, who was almost three years old at the time, walking up the gangway with Stuart. We didn't know at the time that nineteen years later, in 2003, Jeremy would be serving on the *Queen Mary* 2 as Third Officer!

The results were certainly improving; at the Youth Worlds in St Moritz in 1985 Andy Beadsworth won the gold medal in the Laser class. Also in 1985 another Youth Squad member, Lawrence Crispin, won the gold medal in Laser Class World Championships in Sweden and Stuart Childerley took the silver medal.

Girls were included in the Youth World Championships in the late 1980s and in the early 1990s more classes were introduced. So from taking a GBR team consisting of a double-handed and a single-handed dinghy, boys only, we were now taking two double-handed and two single-handed dinghies one crewed by boys and one crewed by girls and we also had a girl and a boy sailing windsurfers. Later still Hobie Cats were included. The World Youth and Women's World Championships were not the only events we succeeded in; we were also winning medals at international regattas in other classes.

As the whole of the Race Training Scheme expanded it became obvious to the politicians of the RYA that we needed more staff to cater for the demand as I was running around ducking and diving, coaching ferrets from Optimist level all the way up to Olympic level. Vernon Stratton, then the Olympic Team Manager, needed more support getting ready for the 1980 Olympic Games, so Peter Bateman was brought in as Olympic Team Coach to help fill the gap on the coaching front.

Peter was brilliant, an excellent helmsman in his own right, a past Fireball World Champion with a vast amount of racing experience at international level and a very good sailmaker. Peter got the team geared up ready for the Moscow Olympic Games and then we were confronted with the huge disappointment of being informed by our favourite politicians that they did not want us to go to the Games. Vernon, Peter and the team were totally devastated, as you can well imagine. After all the hours and money that had been spent in preparation and then not being able to take part was heart breaking news for all concerned, even more so as we had serious medal potential in our team at that time. What was really upsetting after the Games was that some of the GBR athletes ignored the politicians and went anyway, won medals and when they came home were honoured with MBEs. How pathetic was that, rubbing salt into the wounds of those who did as they were asked!

After the disappointment of the Games, more changes were made. The Race Training Scheme had become so big that it was decided by the committees to take it from the Training Division of the RYA and place it under the Racing Division which meant a new boss for me, the one and only John Reed. Like Bob, John was a good boss: he left me to run the scheme unchanged and played a major supporting role which was great. Sally stayed as my secretary, how I'll never know, she must have loved me and all the youth and lady ferrets!

After the debacle of the Moscow Olympics, Peter Bateman left the RYA and John employed Rod Carr as the replacement Olympic Coach in readiness for the Los Angeles Games 1984. Rod came from what was then the National Sailing Centre in Cowes and played a major role in the future development of the RYA Racing Division.

Interlude 5: Coaching To Success

Being successful in anything whether it is education, work, sport or life in general we all need to have a positive attitude about what we are trying to achieve. As I keep reminding myself: positive thinking brings positive results, negative thinking brings negative results; at all times keep yourself surrounded in a positive atmosphere. At the end of each day's training or competing, try to focus on the positive and not the negative.

As I have said many times, prior to any event and after many hours of training, be very realistic about your expectations. I recall one top ferret being interviewed on the television saying that he had entered the event expecting to win and then he was left wondering why he did not.

We would always try to start an event with a good opening result then watch the event unfold, watch what happened to other competitors and keep an eye on the scores. By the end of the event, after all the retirements and disqualifications, there is always a chance you could find yourself on the podium without winning a single race. Motivating those ferrets in the running to win a medal is all about:

- Keeping them focused on their objective
- Learning from any mistakes made on the racecourse
- Eliminating them during their continuing training programme in readiness for the next event
- In order to improve on their personal performance
- And eventually reach the top podium

We all start at the bottom and work our way to the top.

Chapter 9

Developments In Youth Training

After five years of developing the National Race Training Programme at club, regional and national level, it became apparent that, due to the demand for training around the country, the programme had grown too large to be run solely by the staff at RYA headquarters. We therefore put in place a network of Regional Race Training Coordinators, one for each of the RYA regions, including Scotland, Wales and Northern Ireland. These people were tasked with promoting and developing race training for the clubs within their regions who wanted to take part in this national programme. Race training was for both youth and adults carried out by a Club Racing Coach and we organised and ran courses to train those members of the sailing clubs who wished to become racing coaches.

As well as getting the clubs involved, they also organised one Advanced Youth Racing Course during the summer school holidays which would identify top talent within the region and recommend them for the National Youth Squad Training events during the winter. This development became very successful with many youngsters coming through the system into the National Youth Squad. From there many young sailors went on to represent the UK at the World Youth Championships and other national and international regattas.

Some Race Training Coordinators stayed in the role for over a decade producing some really good talent. Richard Watson for the Eastern Region, Gordon Skinner and John Buckingham for the East Midlands, Martin Styles for the South East, Mike Copeland for the South West, Jane Thirwall for Yorkshire and Humberside, John Swanney for the North West, Alan Woolford from the Thames Valley and Valerie Catchpole from the Southern Area to name but a few. All of them put in a huge amount of effort to support youth sailing and identifying top talent.

The job as a Race Training Coordinator was voluntary work, paying only expenses, for which the RYA was very grateful. Without their efforts the whole programme would not have become as successful as it did; we owe them a great deal.

Two other people to whom I owe thanks are Hugh Bailey and Ron Davis. In the early days before we began using video recorders for the debriefs, Hugh would come out with me on the 'mother ship' and would take photographs of rig settings, leach profiles, boat balance and trim both up and downwind, etc. These would be shown on the big screen during the debriefs which was of great benefit to the young sailors. Later Ron Davis came on the scene with an early version of the video recorder, almost the size of a television camera, hoisted on his shoulder in all weather conditions. These were the beginnings of what are now standard debrief sessions at all coaching events.

When I became the National Racing Coach in 1977, I was given a 'company' car. I chose a Ford Cortina Estate as it was a good workhorse for trailing boats and carrying dinghies on the roof with all the gear in the back. As I said previously, I covered many miles and needed a good car. I had three of these in total but in 1982 Ford replaced the Cortina with the Sierra which was not suited to the task. I had a word with John Reed about it and he told me to take time out and find the best replacement. So during the week between training sessions, I test drove all the suitable candidates and decided that the best car on the market to replace the Cortina was a Volvo Estate.

I took delivery of the first Volvo estate, a 240 GL estate

registration A917 RTP, and that was the start of a fantastic relationship with Volvo. These cars were amazing, the amount of weight they could move around made them ideal cars for the job. After the RYA had purchased a couple of Volvos for me from Rudds in Southampton they began talks with Volvo regarding a sponsorship deal. Volvo initially agreed to supply a car for me for the Youth Programme and then extended it to the Olympic Programme and the Olympic Squad. Volvo's support of yachting has carried on ever since, an amazing commitment by Volvo Cars UK and greatly appreciated by all who benefited from it, long may it continue.

During this time with Volvo I carried some heavy loads and someone from Volvo spotted this at one time and organised a photoshoot on the Warsash waterfront of my Volvo 740 with a 420 on the roof and a coach boat behind full of gear and used it on the front cover of one of their brochures to show what the car was capable of doing – it made a good picture. Over a 20-year period I drove well over a million miles of trouble-free motoring and was so impressed that when I left the RYA in the year 2000 I bought my own!

One journey I did in a Volvo was to Rijeka in Yugoslavia in 1989 to the 420 World Championships. I had a 420 on the roof of the car and my Fletcher coach boat on a trailer behind. John Merrick's dad Dennis also drove so the two of us accomplished this epic journey together. On the way I managed to hit a mega pothole and the 420's trolley came through my sunroof. We patched it up with duct tape and luckily Christine was flying out to join me, so she brought a replacement with her.

John had brought a brand new 420 for the regatta and when it went in for measurement, shock and horror, it failed as it had no buoyancy built into it. Not a good start for a regatta. Thankfully the jury allowed us to fill it with inflatable beach balls and after a few hours and a lot of puff we were ready to go. I don't think that you would get away with that today. Moral of the story, never turn up for a major event with an untested brand-new boat. How many times have we said that? We all learn from our mistakes – I hope.

It was a well-attended regatta and we were all accommodated in a hotel. Rijeka was still in a communist country then, so it was quite regimented. The Australian Team were a lively lot and partied most nights, making quite a bit of noise. Our girls decided to have some fun and nipped into the race organiser's office and found some official headed notepaper, typed a letter to the Aussie team informing them that because of the noise they should pack up and leave the hotel. Well pandemonium followed; Huck Scott, the Aussie Team Manager, had the receptionist by the scruff of his neck demanding a refund as the Aussies were beginning to move out! I got wind of what was going on and told Bunny Warren to go and tell the Aussies it was a joke.

We thought that was the end of the matter until a notice was posted on the official noticeboard announcing a jury hearing against Team GBR with regard to Sailing Rule No. 69 – 'Gross Misconduct'. We thought this was the Aussies having a return 'go' at us for what we had done to them and ignored it, but it turned out that we had actually been summoned and the jury secretary came to find me. So there I was at a major event going into a hearing with an Eastern Block jury who were already unhappy because I had not attended at the correct time, trying to explain that this was just a practical joke between the Brits and the Aussies. At the time, we were lying in gold and bronze medal positions with two days to go. I had visions of the whole team being thrown out of the event and me having a great deal of explaining to do to John Reed when we arrived home! Thankfully I managed to convince the jury that this was just a high-spirited prank and, with lots of apologies, we got off with a severe warning – a very lucky escape!

The mid-1980s carried on with the Race Training Scheme evolving all the time with more class associations wishing to be included at club, regional and national level. It was during this time that the Western Australia Yachting Association in Perth asked the Royal Yachting Association for assistance with their Youth Programme and it was decided to send me to assist with some race training sessions at club level over a three week period.

Extract from an Australian newspaper:
SAILING COACH ARRIVES
One of the fittest English exports in years arrived in Perth this week to take up a brief appointment as coach of WA's keen young yachtsmen. Jim Saltonstall has accepted a three-week coaching appointment to improve WA's standing in Australian yachting. He will speak at a State Squad seminar and conduct workshops for Perth sailing clubs during his visit. Mr Saltonstall said that everything from self-preparation to race tactics would be taught to 100 yachting students during his stay in WA.

One of the sessions was to be held in Esperance down on the south coast, so I was driven a thousand miles from Perth. Throughout the whole journey we passed only twelve cars. I remember saying to the driver that back in the UK we would have driven past thousands of cars and sixty million people – he could not comprehend that at all!

It was a useful exercise for me as I learnt from the Aussies and they learnt from me, a beneficial trip all round. It was during this trip that I had the honour of sailing with the Brits on the 12-metre in Fremantle Bay who were preparing *White Crusader* for the America's Cup. I joined Harold Cudmore, Mike Macintyre, Dave Arnold and the team and was given the opportunity to have a go on the helm which was a great experience. On the way back in we were on port tack when a small ferret in an Optimist dinghy hailed 'starboard', making us do a big dial down to miss him! I should think that he was wearing his 'brown corduroy knickers and bicycle clips' at the time!

As president of the RYA, Princess Anne took a great interest in all aspects of the sport in particular both the Olympic and Youth programmes. I remember on one occasion, whilst at the National Youth Championships on Lake Bala, she wanted to go on the water to watch the racing so she came with me in the coach boat. Prior to our boarding the RYA 'Flagship', Princess Anne's security team went on board to check for anything suspicious. Her personal bodyguard was, in my opinion, unaware of how cold it was going to be on the water and I suggested he put on some warmer outer clothing but he was adamant he would be fine.

Having given us a 'clean bill of health' we set off to watch the racing and whilst the ferrets were in between races she wanted to have a chat with some of them, I saw this Laser ferret just sat there with his back towards us and quietly crept up to him. As we came alongside him, he turned around and was very surprised to see the Princess Royal right next to him and said,"Oh hello, how's your mum, you know, the Queen!" Well she just burst out laughing.

Robin Duschene, my boss at the RYA, told me that the Princess had to be back at the clubhouse in time to meet the local VIPs and have lunch. However, she was extremely involved in watching the racing and when I hinted that it was time to return ashore she advised me that she was happy to stay out a while longer. 45 minutes later we eventually made it ashore and we had to help the bodyguard out of the boat as he was almost suffering from hypothermia! Her Royal Highness shook hands with the VIP's and took off in her helicopter. I got it in the ear from Robin Duschene, but it was out of my control!

We had many occasions with Princess Anne over the years as she was always keen to visit events, have a chat with everyone and sometimes award the prizes. On another occasion she came to Queen Mary Sailing Club to present the trophies at a youth event and I happened to have a very young Jeremy with me who was very eager to meet her. He came out on the coach boat with me and on returning to the shore he clung to me like a limpet wanting to speak to her. Eventually, after all the prizes were given out, I introduced him to her as my boatman and she shook his hand and said how pleased she was to meet him and it made his year!! She was always very approachable.

Interlude 6: Working With Parents

Parents, where would we be without them! I would like to think that I developed a special relationship with them and had a great deal of respect for the amount of time, effort, money and mileage that many of them put into ensuring their ferrets were in the right place at the right time for training or attending events.

At the beginning of each year, we would have a parents' meeting during January's winter training programme, and I would map out the plan for the year and established where and when some parents could be of assistance, i.e. towing rescue boats and assisting on the water. It was important to sort out everything early in the programme for everyone involved.

We made it clear that during the training sessions we expected the parents to deliver their ferrets to us and return at the end of the day to collect them; they were not expected to stay and interfere with proceedings. Most ferrets did not want their parents hanging around and giving them 'earache' during their lunch break or from the water's edge! If any parent wished to talk to me they did so over the telephone during the following week. I found that this worked very well.

Chapter 10

Keelboats & Optimists

It was during 1979, when Peter Roberts was Team Manager for the British Admiral's Cup team, that he invited me to talk to the team about the racing rules just to bring them up to speed and answer any questions prior to the event. Ted Heath was in the team and during his campaign I was invited to his house in London to review a protest with him which was very interesting; he was a very hospitable person and we had a nice cup of Yorkshire Tea!

The scheme was going so well that the keelboat sailors started asking for coach support and race training in readiness for their events. The RYA decided it was time to employ a National Keelboat Coach as Rod Carr and myself were too busy with our own programmes to take on any more training. Enter Bill Edgerton, 'Catastrophe Bill' or 'Complicated Bill' as we used to call him! Bill was, and still is, a great bloke even for an Aussie! He worked so hard, sometimes too hard, to sort out all the keelboat ferrets and took his work very seriously. Bill, like the rest of us, put in some serious miles for the keelboat programme as well as getting the new RYA Match Racing Programme off the ground. Match racing was to become an Olympic discipline and so we established a Youth Match Race Training Scheme.

New Zealand, under the leadership of Harold Bennett and the Royal New Zealand Yacht Squadron, launched the unofficial World Youth Match Racing Championships. It was a great success and I'll never know why ISAF (previously IYRU, now

World Sailing) never took it on to make it official so that it could be moved around the world.

I went to Auckland 16 times with the GBR Team which included over the years young sailors like Ian Williams, Adam May, the Sydenham brothers, Ben Vines and many others. On one occasion, the RYA was short of funds and could not afford to send me down with the team, so I went to Heathrow to see them off and wish them good luck. However, the Eric Twiname Trust was generous enough to fund my air fare to enable me to accompany them as their coach. I did not tell them this, so they flew clockwise round, via Singapore, not knowing that I was flying round anti-clockwise, via Los Angeles. I arrived in Auckland just before them and was waiting for them outside arrivals when they emerged. Well, the look on their faces when they came through the door was something else!

That whole series of regattas down under was absolutely great and well organised by Harold and his team under the Royal New Zealand Yacht Squadron flag. Every year I and the three team members were hosted by the same people, Don and Joan Clarke. We became great friends with the whole family, and they deserve a medal the size of a frying pan for putting up with us.

Skippy (Bill's nickname) and I had some great times together at numerous events over the years. Occasionally I would wind him up, as you would expect from a Yorkshireman! I remember a couple of instances, the first whilst we were up at Queen Mary Sailing Club for a match racing event. Skippy had left his car on the upper level next to the club, which was not allowed. So, not missing a chance to upset him, I borrowed a wheel clamp from John Doerr and I wrapped it around the wheel of Skippy's car. I also put one of the club's large stickers over the windscreen, which stated that you should telephone this number to get the car unclamped and it would cost £150!

Shortly, Anne (Bill's secretary at the time) came running in and said, "Have you seen Bill, he is going wild as his car has been clamped and he is in a rush to get away!" (As he always was.) I just kept my head down but, if he had looked closely, he would have seen that the clamp hadn't actually been locked. Needless to say, as time went by, he found out that I did it so I received earache again for half an hour!

On another occasion, we were attending the Royal Lymington Cup Regatta in the western Solent and had both our RIBs tied up to the stern of the mother ship with four knots of tide running at the time. The Race Officer called for Skippy to move the windward mark for him, so Skippy dived into his RIB, having already cast off as you do, not knowing that I had removed the keys from his RIB and there I was, stood on the stern of my RIB, waving them at him as he shot off down tide. I collected him after I had moved the mark and received another half an hour of earache!

One could not resist giving poor Bill a hard time as was the case when Rod Carr and I were southbound together from Birmingham and we received a telephone call (we had mobile phones by then!) from Skippy. As Rod was driving, I answered it. As usual he was in a state, this time because he had just filled his car with petrol when it should have been diesel. He wanted us to help him out but he was in Grafham at the time so I said "No way – and don't put it in your expenses," then put the phone down. Well, the earache we received when we got back into the office, you could hear him down in reception! Good old Skippy, he did a great deal for GBR keelboat racing and was a good egg all-round, I really enjoyed his company and working with him, though I am not sure that those feelings are reciprocated!

I spent the majority of my time out of the office and on the water as you would expect, leaving all the administration to Sally and John Reed: the system worked really well. I remember going to the office on one occasion and the receptionist asking me to 'please sign the visitors' book sir', so I did! I had only been working there for ten years!

When Sally decided to retire she had been my secretary for 11 years so it was a sad day for us to say goodbye. However, our time at Woking was coming to an end anyway as the RYA was outgrowing the building; it was the end of an era. Vivien Warn took over as my secretary and also did an excellent job of looking after the programme, and me, until we were relocated to Eastleigh near Southampton which meant less travelling for me. Vivien decided she did not wish to move to the south coast, and I once again was on the lookout for a new secretary. The RYA was still developing into the largest governing body of sport in the UK. As I mentioned earlier, when I started working for them in 1977 there were 11 members of staff at the office in Woking, when I left in 2000 there were 86 of us. It would appear from the outside looking in, that it was all getting a bit top heavy.

Once again, I was very lucky as Jenny Taylor stepped into the breach! She ran the programme for the next 11 years and, like her predecessors, did an excellent job, taking charge of me as well as all the ferrets! The Youth Squad was getting bigger and stronger in performance terms and another person who came into the mix and really helped us along was Dr Frank Newton. He spent hours sorting out their fitness training, testing and generally supporting the programme in committee and in race management, acting as Race Officer down in Weymouth with his infamous yacht *Sorebones*. His wife Jenni used to keep Frank on the straight and narrow, supporting him on board and assisting with running all the races. Jenni was also brilliant at churning out cups of Yorkshire Tea as required!

It was in the late 1980s when we put more focus on the Optimist class. Even though they had been involved from the beginning, the RYA thought that we should focus on involving them at a slightly higher level of race training between the ages of eleven to fourteen. So, over the following ten years, I travelled to the Optimist National and International Championships with the GBR Optimist Teams as their coach. This is when I met up with Phil Slater, an Optimist coach from Restronquet Sailing Club in Falmouth. Phil had a group of excellent ferrets training in Falmouth some of who I took to the World Championships in various countries during that ten-year time frame. Names like Iain Percy, David Lenze, Jamie Shelton, Ben Ainslie, Chris Draper, Sian Maddocks, Nick Rogers, Bart Simpson and numerous others were involved before going on to the senior youth classes such as the Laser and 420.

Like all the other youth classes we were involved with, there was a selection scheme to ascertain which 'ferrets' would represent the class in international events. This selection was carried out by the Optimist Committee mainly made up of parents. I have recently discovered this article written by a very observant Optimist sailor having a dig at the whole procedure. It is very amusing:

The Selection

And there came upon the land the time of the 'Selection'. And all the families did prepare their children. And they did choose from amongst their number a representative to be their leader, as is written. And they did choose Paul Hobbs, son of James. And Paul did leave his chosen people and climb the mountain and whence after much travel and endless committee meetings he did reach the summit and he did see JIM. And Paul did fall to the earth and tremble in fear and JIM did speak unto Paul in a voice which shook the earth, and he did instruct him of the sacred duties of the Chairman. And as he did speak he did inscribe his words upon a tablet of stone and his words were thus:

Thou shalt accept all blame for all decisions even if they are not of thy making

Thou shalt not slumber until all of thy Optimist paperwork is completed

Thou shalt spend at least half thy waking hours upon the telephone

---

> *Thou shalt never become enraged at thy chosen people even at the time of Selection*
>
> And JIM bade Paul to rise, take the tablets and spread the joyful news amongst his chosen people. However, when Paul didst return from the mountain, his eyes did behold a terrible sight – A great carnage was before him as the parents did fight over the offsprings' results and upon seeing this sight anger welled from his soul and his voice did rent the air:
> "Oh foolish parents, Oh untrusting Philistines"
> He did then tear asunder the results and dash the tablets to the ground and the tablets did break into a thousand fragments. And Paul did once more leave the parents and did climb the mountain. At the top of the mountain he found JIM, and JIM did once more speak in a voice that shook the ground and he did say:
> "WELL PAUL THAT'S LIFE IN A BLUE SUIT – YOU KNOW WHAT I MEAN!"
>
> From the book of Optimus, attributed to Mark, son of Paul

As with most youngsters when they travel together as a team you have to keep an eye on them, and we were due to go to the World Championships in Argentina a few years after the Falklands War so I questioned John Reed as to whether or not we should be going. The RYA politicians said that we should go as it would be seen as a good public relations exercise between the UK and Argentina and so we went.

Mar Del Plata was the venue which was an awesome place to sail, with big Atlantic rollers breaking close to the entrance of the marina. We were all briefed to follow a narrow channel out of the entrance so as to avoid the breaking waves; however, a Swedish ferret decided to stray out of the channel, got caught by a breaking wave and capsized. His coach dashed in with the RIB to rescue him and was also capsized, both boats ending up on the beach; fortunately, they both survived. No one else made the same mistake during the rest of the event!!

All the ferrets were also briefed not to throw food into the water as there were a large number of seals in the area. Now Nick Rogers, being Nick Rogers, had to feed the seals only to end up with a seal in his boat – just as well that he was wearing his brown corduroy knickers and bicycle clips!!

I briefed the team, which included Ben Ainslie, Chris Draper and Nick Rogers, that this was going to be a very low-key event for us, to keep a low profile, no incidents, don't attract attention to ourselves and just get on with the sailing.

We got to our hotel which was at the junction of two major roads, sorted out the rooms and then I became aware of a disturbance outside. When I looked out of the window, I saw a massive crowd of football supporters who were returning from seeing Argentina beat Brazil and they were pointing up to our window shouting abuse. I went into the ferrets' room and there they were throwing water bombs at them and waving the union jack out of the window. Well, as you can imagine, I went 'ape shape' and had to do a great deal of apologising to prevent an international incident!

In that same year, Ben went on to win the gold medal in the Laser Radial World Championships in New Zealand. This whole group of young sailors were going to be the superstars of the future, winning between them numerous European, World and Olympic medals.

The pinnacle of our successes in the World Youth Championships came in 1995 in Bermuda when GBR won gold medals in the Laser Two class courtesy of Nick Rogers and Pom Green (Boys) and Jessie and Sally Cuthbert (Girls) and

Ben Ainslie also won gold in the Laser One class. The GBR Team won the Volvo / Nautica Cup for the best team. After their performance in Bermuda, the Youth Team was again voted Yachtsmen of the Year at the London Boat Show as, previously mentioned, having won it in 1984. Ben Ainslie went on to the Olympics the following year in Atlanta and won the silver medal.

We won the Volvo Youth Trophy / Nautica Cup again in 1996 in Newport Rhode Island when Jessie and Sally Cuthbert again won gold and Chris Draper and Dan Newman won silver also in the Laser Two. At the Youth Worlds in 1996, Sally Cuthbert won her fourth gold medal in a row, an amazing achievement yet to be repeated by a dinghy sailor anywhere in the world. Sally set the benchmark for others to follow.

Interlude 7: Dealing With Prime Donnas

Prima donnas are talked about in sport, but in my world they do not exist. To me they are the same as anyone else and are treated as such. If they make a mistake, they do 20 press-ups just like the rest.

If I am working with sailors who are at the pinnacle of their careers, I come out of the coaching mode and into the support role. I become the eyes and ears of the programme, looking and listening and adding any constructive information about their performance ready for the next race.

Chapter 11

My Own Sailing

My position as National Racing Coach didn't confine me to coaching young sailors, my services could be called upon by any club or class association, as happened on numerous occasions. On one occasion I was asked by the 505 class to support their team at the World Championships in Helsinki.

All the boats were shipped out and the ferrets flew out, leaving me to drive to Finland towing the coach boat. It was yet another nice journey, driving up to Trevemunde then catching the Finnjet across to Helsinki. I was very impressed with the ship which did 30 knots – reminded me of my time in the Royal Navy doing the same speed in both frigates and destroyers.

On arrival in Helsinki, I realised that I was the only one there with a car so, needless to say, I became the team taxi. I had ten ferrets to ferry around and on one particular morning we were pushed for time, so we managed to squash most of them into the Volvo and Bill Masterman, who is seven feet tall, was placed across the back seat with his head outside the port-side rear window and his feet outside the starboard rear window! We were heading for the club and we heard a police siren and I saw blue lights flashing in my rear mirror. Sure enough we were pulled over by 'Mr Plod' who could not believe how many ferrets were in this Volvo and that the head out of the port window belonged to the feet out of the starboard window. Needless to say, I had to offload some ferrets and then do a return trip from the club to pick up the rest. Fortunately, 'Mr Plod' saw the funny side and let me off with a caution. Yet another occasion when I breathed a sigh of relief!

I also managed to squeeze in some personal racing and one year, in the early eighties, John Oakley was kind enough to lend me his Soling, which was sat on its trailer in a very sorry state behind the shed belonging to the sailmakers Miller and Whitworth. Neil Macdonald, who had been a member of the Youth Squad, and Pat Lilley, a friend from the yachting industry, came along as crew.

It took us quite a long time to sort out the boat, which basically needed a full refit, but we managed to get it reasonably ship-shape and after a few hours of practice out in the Solent, we had enough boat handling skills for entry into Weymouth Olympic Week. I was on the helm, Neil was bowman and Pat was the middle man. On one occasion, during tacking practice, whilst Pat was hiking out, the wire strop clipped to his hiking harness snapped. Well, his legs shot vertically in the air up the side of the boat and his hands were in the handles preventing him from falling overboard but he couldn't get himself back inboard. As Pat was a big man, both Neil and I could not lift him back in so the only thing to do was to tack and float him back inboard. Needless to say, Mr Lilley was not amused, his words, mostly unrepeatable, could be heard right across the Solent. Of course, both Neil and I were laughing so much, which didn't help! We did have some laughs sailing that boat and we got some good results during Weymouth Week, upsetting some of the top ferrets as the week went on.

I also had the honour and pleasure of teaming up with my old mate Eddie Warden Owen as tactician onboard the J24 class *Luder*, along with Adrian Friend, Brian Hodge, Andy Hemmings and a hooligan by the name of Ossie Stewart. We had a great time campaigning *Luder* both on and off the water, winning the National Championships in Poole and Brighton and finishing second at the World Championships in Japan. We were very disappointed to say the least that we did not win the gold medal as all we had to do was beat Kenny Read from the USA in the last race. At the start of the last beat, we had him well covered when, out of the blue, the wind collapsed, filling in slowly from 180 degrees and Kenny sailed past us with the spinnaker up just before we crossed the line. We were gutted. I blame the tactician!

We then went on to win the Southern Area Championships with me as the helm because Ed could not be with us. I also sailed in the Northern Area Championships on *Jitterbug* with both Gary and Mike Kaye, another pair of hooligans, which we also won. During 1990 I finished my J24 sailing as European Champion, crewing for Jim Brady along with Andy Hemmings in Kiel; I was tactician and a good time was had by all.

One of the highlights of my time whilst racing on *Luder*, was during the World Championships at Poole on a day when it was blowing forty knots, going downwind with the spinnaker up. Two boats sank that day and I have to admit we were wearing our brown corduroy trousers and bicycle clips, especially when it came to getting the spinnaker down ready to round the leeward mark. How we never sank I will never know!!

Another personal sailing experience I enjoyed came in June 1994. It was the fiftieth anniversary of the Normandy landings (D-Day) and the south coast put on a fine display with a fleet review. I had been invited by a good friend of mine, Guy Shackles from the Royal Yorkshire Yacht Club who was Master of the training ship *Royalist*, to sail on her at the review in the Solent. I took along with me three good friends, Bob Dunningham and Pete Bowler who were ex Royal Navy and Peter Falconer. Guy sailed on *The Prospect of Whitby* with Arthur Slater for many years, competing in many Admiral's Cup events, and was a top racing ferret.

We had a great three days on board, especially climbing the rigging which reminded me of my days at HMS *Ganges*. We sailed from Gosport to Poole in a fresh westerly wind and had a very good 'run ashore' before progressing east through the Solent to our review position off Spithead, ready to give three cheers to 'Betty' as she sailed past in the Royal Yacht *Britannia* before she left for the coast of Normandy to take part in the commemorations. We returned to Gosport to disembark and headed home for a recovery period, what a great weekend!

Chapter 12

The Olympics

Having progressed through the Youth Programme, the next logical step was into the Olympics which many of them did with great success winning medals first of all in Atlanta and thereafter at all the following Games. In 1996 I had the honour of being asked to be the Olympic Team Coach for GBR, and I was delighted to accept.

Extract written by Andrew Preece from Yachting World:

The mission statement of the 1996 British Olympic team management is to 'Bring back more medals than any other previous team we have sent to the Games', and the man upon whose shoulders that responsibility rests is Team Coach Jim Saltonstall.

You have to go back to 1908 in the Olympic record books to find the last time that Britain was the top performer at the Olympic sailing regatta. That was nineteen Games ago in which time the Americans have topped the bill seven times, Sweden three times, Norway twice and a handful of other nations once. As a nation of sailors our record, particularly in recent years, has been disappointing... But this year the atmosphere is different. There's a feeling in the air that this British team could achieve something special, a collective spirit that if not inspired by Team

Coach Jim Saltonstall, has been tangibly catalysed by him. "I personally will be very disappointed if we didn't come away with some medals... of whatever colour. I think we have the sailors that are capable of doing that."

These Games were quite a challenge, as we knew they would be, with the racing areas being off the coast of Savannah. The tides were very tricky with many changes in both direction and strength as all race areas were close to a large river estuary. As Rod Carr, who was appointed as our Team Manager, had done his homework meticulously we were well prepared for the coming events, so we knew that if things went our way, we stood a chance of some medals.

Rod had put together a great support team, good accommodation and we had a strong team of ferrets. Our accommodation was a 45-minute RIB ride to the marina which was close to the river entrance, and this made for long days by the time we returned in the evening. Also the conditions were extremely difficult: hot and humid and the ferrets were drinking up to 15 litres of liquid a day in order to keep hydrated. The weather was also an issue with thunderstorms never far away. Prior to the start of the event, we had to evacuate the marina as a hurricane started to roll towards us, but fortunately it passed without causing too much damage, allowing us to continue with our preparations.

As always at any major sailing event we had our 'ups and downs', but we had two great results. John Merricks and Ian Walker won the silver medal in the 470 by beating the Portugese ferrets in the last race. Ben Ainslie, after winning his gold medal at the Youth Worlds in Bermuda, took silver after an excellent performance at the age of nineteen – a fantastic result for such a young man and, as we now know, this was just the beginning. Shirley Robertson just missed the bronze medal which was very

disappointing for her after a fine effort; however, the experience set her up for next Games in Sydney.

Great Britain had a poor Olympic Games in Atlanta and, if I remember correctly, only won four medals, two of which were in the sailing team. The Chairman of the British Olympic Association, Craig Reedie, came down to Savannah for the medal ceremony and took all the GBR Sailing Team out for dinner and I will never forget that, when he put his credit card on the table to pay, he said "Thank goodness you lot did alright!"

When we arrived home our budget went from approximately £70,000 to £2.3million ready for the next Games – success does bring its rewards! This extra funding set us up for a successful Olympics in Sydney 2000.

In the New Year's Honours List at the end of 1996, Queen Elizabeth (Betty!) was kind enough to award me an MBE for services to the sport and young people. I was 'over the moon' to receive such an award and I was so pleased that I actually received my medal from Her Majesty at Buckingham Palace and shook her hand. I squeezed her hand so tightly that her eyeballs rolled around in their sockets!

David Seaman was in the queue behind me, and we got chatting. He complained the whole time about Liverpool being awarded a penalty against him even though Robbie Fowler (from Liverpool) told the referee that David had not fouled him. He was most upset as Liverpool won 2-1 and the penalty decided the match.

It was a fantastic experience, I even dressed up in a top and tails and Christine and Jeremy came along to watch the ceremony.

Having never driven out of Buckingham Palace before, I got to the gates and, as it is such a wide road and there was no traffic at the time, I turned right. Suddenly Christine shouted, "I think this a one-way system and we're going the wrong way!" At that time, the traffic lights that had been holding up the traffic turned green, and we were faced with an oncoming charge of black cabs. I've never executed a U-turn as quickly as I did that day. Christine and Jeremy had sunk down in their seats with embarrassment! From that time on I was addressed by friends and colleagues as 'The Queen's Peasant', and it's a title that I continue to use.

The following year, 1997, was a sad one as we lost one of our top racing ferrets – John Merricks, in a road traffic accident. John was one of the best sailors in the country at that time. I took him to two Youth World Championships, Barcelona in 1986 and Montreal in 1987, as well as to various 420 and 470 events, where he was always in the top end of the fleet. The climax being his silver medal at the Atlanta Olympics. He had a wicked sense of humour and was always up to some mischief with me not far behind trying to sort him out. I remember when a 20-foot inflatable penguin went missing at the 470 Worlds in Argentina it was never found. His funeral was held at Leicester Cathedral, and it was full to capacity he was such a popular young man, sadly missed.

Whilst remembering John, I must also mention the sad losses of Glyn Charles who was lost overboard during the Sydney to Hobart Race, in extreme weather conditions, and Andrew 'Bart' Simpson who was a member of the Swedish America's Cup team who was thrown from the catamaran during a race and also Simon Russell 'Fumesy' who died recently at home due to the dreaded Covid 19. More recently we lost Sam Richmond who died whilst racing off Antigua. They were five very talented ferrets of mine, I hope that they all found a safe anchorage.

Over the next four-year period all of our race training programmes, squads and teams progressed well. I was still doing an average of 40,000 miles a year, still driving Volvos, as well as goodness knows how many miles in aeroplanes! Over the years, although I had mostly trouble-free driving with regard to reliability of my cars, I did have the odd mishap.

Driving home late one night in my Cortina, after giving a talk in Dover, I hit black ice and skidded off into a ditch. It was a freezing cold night and I climbed out and went to look for help. I found an isolated house and woke up the owner and asked if he would ring the police for me and waited at the gate for someone to arrive. When help turned up we drove back to my car and on the way he pointed out some tracks heading into a field saying this must be it. They weren't my tracks, I was further along the road, they belonged to a Porsche which had also come off the road and was upside down in the field. Thankfully for this guy he would now get rescued, because had I not gone into the ditch, he would never have been found. My car was towed out of the ditch, and I climbed back in and drove home!

On another occasion, driving in the East Midlands with Gordon Skinner, who was our regional co-ordinator for the area, I crashed the Volvo into a brick wall. We came off a right-angle bend on black ice, again, the car lost traction and T-boned the wall. The bonnet was pushed up in the air and the front lights were pointing towards the sun. I got out, kicked the front tyre in frustration as you do, looked at it, got back in, turned the key and it started – good old Volvo! I then jumped up and down on the bonnet to flatten it out so that I could see over the top of it, dropped Gordon off and drove it back home. The next day I took it to the Volvo garage in Southampton and my mechanic John looked at it and said, "What did you hit?" When I told him that I had been through a brick wall, he could not believe that I had driven it all the way back from Matlock in Derbyshire in such a mess. It cost £2,000 to rebuild. Gordon named the corner 'Jim's corner'; it reminds me of him every time I pass it.

Talking about scary car moments, when I was driving from Genoa during the night through France returning from the Women's World Championships in Sardinia with a 420 on the roof and a coach boat behind with a car full of girls, the time came to change drivers. One of the girls, whose name I won't mention, took over. I had just nodded off in the passenger seat when, all of a sudden, I woke up because the car was swerving violently from side to side. I grabbed the wheel and shouted to accelerate which she did and fortunately we came out of it and survived. We found out from the rest of the team, who had been following on behind us, that the motorway traffic had all slowed right down or even stopped as it looked as if we were going to roll over. Not a nice feeling at all. I am pleased to say that we did make it home safely in the end.

On another occasion on my return home from Kiel Week with the Youth Team, again with a 420 on the roof and coach boat behind with two Lasers inside, I reached the old Hockley traffic lights near Winchester and, as I slowed down, I noticed that there was an 'Evil Knievel' policeman following me on his motorbike. As I stopped, he pulled up alongside, tapped on the window and said, "Do you realise sir that you were doing 55mph and that your trailer was swerving all over the place." So I looked him in the eye and said, "Officer you should see it when I'm doing 90mph!" Thankfully he had a good sense of humour (must have been born in Yorkshire!) and laughed and let me carry on!

Considering the number of miles I covered over the years, I was very lucky to have so few mishaps and no injuries.

Whilst we were at the London Boat Show in January 2000, I was on the RYA stand when the Minister for Sport appeared for a visit and he asked me, "How many medals will the Sailing Team win this time?" To which I replied, "Three gold" and he said, "I'll hold you to that."

Again, Rod Carr gathered together a great onshore team and our accommodation was perfect, really close to the marina saving us having to travel to and from the Olympic Village which was good for the ferrets' morale. This was another major event with 'ups and downs' but with more 'ups' than 'downs'!

Success came with Ben Ainslie in the Laser class with a classic last race; Ben and Robert Scheidt were both in contention for the gold medal and Ben did a great 'match-race' manoeuvre on

Robert. This went to a protest meeting and as I had managed to see the aerial video footage in the BBC caravan this helped us to prepare a good case for the jury and Ben won the gold! We carried Ben up the launching ramp ashore whilst still sat in his Laser!

Ian Walker and Mark Covell took the silver medal in the Star class, just missing the gold medal by one point, so close! Shirley Robertson also won gold in the Europe class and Andy Barker with Simon Hiscocks won silver in the 49er class in its debut Olympic Games. Andy Beadsworth, Barry Parkin and Richard Sydenham had a tough week in the Soling class. After successfully qualifying in the fleet racing to go through to the match racing, they lost out to the German team who then went on to win the silver medal in the final match. Nick Rogers and Joe Glanfield missed the bronze medal by one point in the 470 class – very disappointing for all concerned having performed really well all week.

So we won three gold and two silver medals which made us Great Britain's highest medal winning team at the Sydney Olympic Games. Job done! The medal ceremony for the sailing events was held on the steps of the Sydney Opera House and it was fantastic: we sang the British National Anthem that many times and so loud that we lost our voices – I have never been so proud in my life.

I sat down at the medal ceremony, took a few seconds to reflect and said to myself, "The last 23 years have been well worth it." I saw this as the apex of my coaching career, time to retire!

We certainly celebrated at the closing ceremony which was a wonderful occasion for all of us. I'll never forget when the fighter plane came swooping into the arena, stubbing out the Olympic flame as it passed over the top of it. Then, in the middle of the stadium, standing on its tail, taking off like a rocket and passing over the bridges along the river, each one exploding with fireworks. And finally, over the harbour bridge which really set alight with a fantastic display as the plane pointed in the direction of Greece as if to return the flame. Amazing, a good time was had by all. The closing party was awesome with Kylie performing on stage – I think the whole Great British Team had a thoroughly good time!

Afterwards Christine and I stayed in Australia for a holiday and visited the Great Barrier Reef and the Blue Mountains for three weeks and had a very nice relaxing time. When I left for Australia to take part in the Olympics, we were told to bring very little baggage as we would all be issued with the team uniform and bags. We assembled in Brisbane and were suited and booted with everything we needed including suitcases, amazing. So, when it came to leaving Australia and returning home, I arrived at the airport still wearing 'Team GB' kit as that was all the clothing I had to wear! The lady at the British Airways check-in desk said, "Oh Team GB, which sport?" When I said 'sailing', she commented that the sailing team had done very well. I cheekily said, "Yes, we should be travelling back in First Class", so she went away and came back with two tickets for Business Class all the way back to London. What a fantastic way to end the perfect visit to Australia, never to be forgotten.

It was shortly after that Rod Carr told me that the RYA was about to restructure for all the right reasons. Also, once again, it had outgrown itself and was going to move to new larger premises in Hamble. In the restructuring programme he said that there would no longer be any permanent coaches on the staff and so it was time to go.

I was very disappointed and sad to leave after 23 great years working with some great people. Jenny Taylor had decided to retire and for my final few months Kath O'Connell ran the programme with me, also doing a great job. The RYA looked after me very well indeed on my departure and I shall look back on those 23 years as some of the best in my life. To have worked with some of the best sailors this country has produced has been a great privilege and an honour for me.

Chapter 13

Going Freelance

The new millennium kicked off with GBR sailing on top of the world and as a freelance self-employed coach, I was left wondering what was around the corner. Both Christine and I were amazed at how quickly the word had spread around the sailing community that I was now freelancing, and the phone started to ring! It meant I was still putting in the mileage around the UK and abroad although I knew in my heart that I could not go and work for another nation. We had put in so much effort over the past 23 years to make GBR so competitive in the sailing world and, having been rewarded by 'Betty', it would not have been right to then go and help the opposition.

The ISAF (now World Sailing) contacted me and asked if I would do the job as their International Youth Coach. This involved helping young ferrets from other countries that needed some help and support at the ISAF World Youth Championships which was not being provided by their home National Authorities. I accepted the job and did it until 2008, when I had attended my 30th Youth World Championship – a nice round number to retire on. ISAF very kindly awarded me a Lifetime Achievement Award and their silver medal for services to the sport; the end of another era.

Extract from announcement by ISAF
Jim Saltonstall was honoured on Thursday night at the Volvo Youth Sailing ISAF Youth World Championship

after 30 years during which he has coached some of the greatest names in the sport. There have been many legendary sailing names to emerge from the Volvo Youth Sailing ISAF World Championship; names who have gone on to win Olympic gold medals, lift the America's Cup and triumph in the Volvo Ocean Race. Few of them have passed under the radar of British coach Jim Saltonstall, who during 30 years at the championship has made an immeasurable contribution to youth sailing, first of all in Great Britain and latterly on a worldwide scale. On the occasion of his 30th and final ISAF Youth Sailing World Championship, Jim Saltonstall was honoured for his incredible achievements at the event.

Also in the early stages of self-employment, Stuart Childerley turned up like a bad penny! A top racing ferret, and all-round good egg, he was campaigning to win a gold medal at the Etchell World Championships which were to be held in Christchurch Bay and asked if I would help him, Simon Russell (Fumesy) and Nick Pearson to achieve this. So we began working on the ten aspects of the most challenging sport in the world and succeeded in winning the gold medal. It was a great result in a very competitive fleet which included Dennis Conner who had, coincidentally, presented Stuart with his World Youth gold medal back in 1984 in San Diego.

We enjoyed it so much that we went to New Zealand the following year, with Roger Marino on the bow this time, and won it again with a day to spare in what was a very windy event with 30 knots of wind every day – only the fittest will win!

We went to the USA the following year, hoping to make it a 'hat trick', but finished fifth in very light and difficult conditions. Stuart then left the Etchell programme as a helm but carried on sailing with others as a very experienced crew member.

The next 'ex-ferret' to request coaching support was Andy Beadsworth, another Laser World Youth Championship gold medallist which he won in Switzerland 1985. He had also started racing in the Etchell class with Simon Fry and Oscar Strugstad and wanted to win the gold medal at the Etchell World Championships, this time in the Solent. So, as with Stuart, we began our training programme and once again, I'm pleased to say, we won the gold medal.

By now I was spending most of my time in the keelboat scene with ferrets who, not too many years ago, were either in the GBR Youth Programme or the Olympic Team or both. It was great to see how far so many of them had progressed in their sailing lives and, as we had known each other for many years, they knew what to expect!

The America's Cup is the only major trophy we have yet to win and the current team trying to achieve this is made up mainly of youngsters who came through the RYA Youth, Olympic and Keelboat programmes. As previously mentioned, it was the RYA establishing the keelboat programme run by Bill Edgerton that has led to our keelboat sailors' successes.

I was also contacted by my good friend Edward Warden Owen who had recently been employed by the Royal Ocean Racing Club as their Chief Executive Officer. Ed, as I have mentioned previously, was a top racing ferret and coach – one of the best in the UK – and whom I have competed against and with over many years. He was a member of the GBR team selected to represent us in the 470 class at the Moscow Games in 1980. However, of course, he didn't get to attend.

Ed was hoping to offer coaching to any yachts that had entered for the RORC Easter Regatta and asked me if I was interested in being involved with the coaching. We were offering coaching to the helms and crews of the competing yachts who were looking to improve their skills in readiness for future events. In order to meet the demand, I teamed up with Barry (Stunning) Dunning, another good mate of mine and an experienced sailor and coach. The idea was that over the three-day weekend between us we would offer advice and assistance during the racing to all those who requested it followed by a video debrief each evening. It was a great success and has carried on now for the past 15 years. Hopefully it will continue as there are numerous ferrets out there requiring advice to speed up their learning curve. I recall one team saying to me that they had learnt more in three days than they had the whole of their previous season.

Being involved in this programme led me on to the TP52 circuit. Brendan Darrer asked me if I would be interested in working with him on his TP52 project *Cristabella*. I spent five great years working with him and his exceptional team. They were an awesome bunch, all professional sailors from different sailing backgrounds. I was there to facilitate and support them in what they wanted to achieve and did not consider myself the team coach as they did not need coaching, just supporting. All the crew were at the apex of their game, I would say to them, "You may be the best in the world at what you do, but after each regatta, ask yourself, how can I do my job better?" As professional sailors, that is the only way forward.

John Cook was the owner of the boat, a great guy who really enjoyed his racing as an amateur helmsman, often beating the top professional skippers around him. We competed in the Audi Med Cup circuit for five years, against many of the best sailors in the world which was a great experience. In the early days of the programme there would be 22 boats racing in very close situations with not much room for error. Any collisions that did occur were very expensive, just like F1 motor racing.

John used to call me 'Yorkshire' and sometimes he would hop aboard the RIB between races and say "now then 'Yorkshire', how are we doing?" and have a sneaky fag! One day he jumped in and said, "'Yorkshire' I've had a great race, we went round the windward mark ahead of Ben Ainslie!" As an amateur owner driver, that made his day – he was 'over the moon'. He was a great man surrounded by an excellent team,. Sadly, the programme came to an end in 2010 when John became rather ill, but we all enjoyed sailing and working with him and it was sad to lose this great character from the sport.

During an event in Palma, Majorca the volcano in Iceland erupted. With no flights from Majorca back to the UK, a few of us, who had to get back home for other sailing commitments, looked at the weather map and as it showed a settled forecast. We made the decision to make the crossing from Majorca to Valencia in *Cristabella*'s RIB. Five of us climbed in and 'legged' it at 30 knots the whole way which took us five hours, the longest RIB ride I have ever done!

The sea was absolutely flat calm all the way to Valencia. Dougal had organised to pick up a hire a car at the airport but when we got there, he was told that they had let his car go to another customer. He had obviously been offered more money! Well Dougal, one of our grinders on *Cristabella* and a big lad, went ballistic and grabbed the agent by the scruff of his neck, dragged him over the counter and demanded the car he had booked be brought to him immediately! Without further ado a car was produced which was a bigger and better car than the one he booked! We drove all night to the northern coast of France where we had booked a passage on the cross-channel ferry and met up with some other Brits, Tim Powell and his team, who were going to Spain for a sailing event and passed on the car to them to take back to Valencia. We boarded the ferry and made it back to the UK! What an epic trip that was.

Chapter 14

More Coaching & Sailing

Whilst we were in Perth Australia January 2007 at the Etchell Worlds with Stuart Childerley we came up with the idea of a mega reunion to celebrate 30 years of both the Youth and Women's squads. Christine and Lisa Childerley agreed to take on the organisation of the event to be held at the Royal Southern Yacht Club. It was open to anyone who had been involved in RYA youth and women's training since the birth of the scheme in 1977. Along with all the ferrets who had passed through the scheme we included those who initiated it, so Bob Bond and John Reed came along, and all three of my secretaries. It was great to see them all together, and others who had been instrumental in its success.

What a night it turned out to be: over 200 ferrets turned out in their best 'bib and tucker' for a fantastic reunion. It was great to see so many faces from the past, many of them now European, World and Olympic Champions. They really enjoyed it and I think it would have gone on all night if the Royal Southern staff had allowed it! It was scary to learn the following day some ferrets crossed over to Warsash during the night on windsurfers and canoes after a skin full. Nothing changes as we have seen it all before, at home and abroad!!

During the first decade of the new millennium, I was kept very busy with a variety of projects. The International 420 Class Association asked me to run some International Coaches Seminars around the world, which turned out to be well supported. The furthest west we have been is Los Angeles and the furthest east was to Japan and everywhere in between including Russia in 2012 (it took me three trips to London and £100 to get a visa – never again!). This was a real eye opener; I was given my own armed bodyguard who drove me around in a large Mercedes 4x4 with black tinted windows for the week! The driving over there is manic – they think nothing of driving onto the pavement to overtake, there are no such things as speed limits – hairy stuff, very educational! The seminar was held on the River Volga in the middle of Russia, the sailing centre was something else, the best I have ever seen. They had everything you could ever wish for as a training facility; the Russians have spent a lot of money to produce top ferrets, the Russians are coming!

The next project to come along was Andy Beadsworth with a Dragon class project. Andy, Jamie Lea and the owner Klaus Diederichs wanted to win the Dragon Worlds in Weymouth, so off we went again with a full-on training programme and another gold medal which was awesome. It was the toughest World Championship that I have ever witnessed. We won by one point on the last beat of the last race which involved a photo finish between a Ukrainian and a Russian. We did not know that we had won until we were informed when we arrived at the dock.

What made this gold medal so special was that on day three of the event we were involved in an incident with a Swedish boat at the windward mark which I managed to catch on video. When we got ashore Klaus was not really bothered about going ahead with the protest, so I whispered in his port shell-like ear that if he did not go ahead with it he might regret it at the end of the event. As suggested, he went ahead with the protest which he won and therefore gained one point as the Swede had finished one place ahead of us and that point alone gave us the gold medal – another lesson learnt. Consequently that led up to yet another celebration and headache after I fell down the stairs back at our accommodation! Andy went on to win two further Dragon World Championships, a completely awesome performance.

More was to come in the Etchell class with Stuart, Fumesy and Roger winning the European Championships followed by the Nationals. This led to more celebrations at the end of which we were invited to leave the restaurant in Cowes as we were not a pretty sight. The less said the better as when I arrived home the following day I was still covered in red wine, Christine was not impressed!

As we moved on through the noughties and into the following decade the jobs kept on coming in. I continued to work with Klaus, Grant Gordon and Andy in both the Dragon and the Swan 45 programmes all over Europe. I also kept my connections with the 420 class, conducting 420 Class Coaching Seminars with my good friend from Portugal, Jose Massapina, and also attending their European and World Championships to carry out video and debrief sessions. Ed also insisted that I carry on working with him at the RORC Easter Challenge weekends. So there has never been a dull moment, always like a coiled spring ready for action either at home or abroad flying the flag for both Betty (The Queen) and Annie (The Princess Royal) and the County of Yorkshire!

As I mentioned earlier, during my time working as a coach I travelled extensively by car to various events, averaging around 40,000 miles per annum and amongst these were some epic journeys. There was the one I talked about earlier to Yugoslavia with Dennis Merricks towing the coach boat and carrying the 420 on the roof. Another was to Gdynia in Poland for the World Youth Championships when I was working as the International Youth Coach.

Christine and I decided to drive there in order to visit Berlin, a city we both wanted to see. We stayed overnight in Holland and then a couple of nights in Berlin and on to the Polish border.

We had enjoyed the Dutch and German motorways en route and could not believe the state of the roads once we crossed the border – they turned into a tank track, the first few miles being on cobbled roads! We had an exciting journey as the Polish drivers were pretty 'gung-ho'!

Again, when I was asked by the 420 Association to attend the Europeans in Hungary on Lake Balaton, we decided to make the journey by car as we had purchased a Volvo C70 convertible and wanted to give it a good run in Europe. We had another great drive passing through some great scenery. On our way home we went to Italy to work with Klaus Dietrich and his team on *Fever* in Orbetello, just north of Rome. This was not long after they had suffered a major earthquake and it was very eerie driving along passing crumpled buildings and on such quiet and badly damaged roads. One place we passed was a car showroom and all the cars were still on the forecourt with the remains of the building on top of them

Over the past few years I have had the pleasure of twice being invited to take part in 'The Round the Island Race', with the one and only Bob Fisher in his scaled down version of *Shamrock* called *Rosenn*. What a fantastic yacht and what a motley crew he brought together: Bob, Barry Dunning, Alan Warren, Eddy Warden Owen and me. What a great experience that was, a laugh from start to finish!

On one of the races we did, I was on the helm approaching the Needles and I said to Bob, "Shall we go inside the wreck?" Bob had on one occasion gone aground on that wreck! I cannot repeat what the answer was, so we took the safe passage! As we approached St Catherine's it was heading towards midday – TOT time – and I had brought the traditional hip flask full of Woods rum. Our cabin boy produced the tot glasses and, as one does at midday, we proposed a toast to Betty (The Queen). The tots went down in one and Bob looked at me and said, "By that was good Jim, we shall have to wash it down with a nice bottle of wine!" By the time we got round to Ryde, *Rosenn*'s course was like that of a merchant ship dodging U-boats in the Atlantic during World War Two!

On another occasion we were round the back of the island in a good breeze with wind over tide and more than once we had to send Barry up forward to set the A sail, *Rosenn* did not have much freeboard so, with all his weight up there, the bow kept dipping, sending the wet stuff back aft and I was sounding the klaxon as if we were about to dive! If we had she would have gone straight down as she was a very heavy yacht. By 'eck we did have a great time sailing together, lots of laughs which is what it is all about, sailing is fun!

Another Round the Island Race was with my brother Dick who was skippering *Gipsy Moth IV.* She was a heavy boat on the helm to sail with all that weight and only a small rudder. My arms were twice the size by the end of the day! So we had two Saltonstalls once again on the same boat, a definite recipe for trouble! As we rounded Bembridge for the leg home we were close-hauled on port tack in approximately fifteen knots of wind heading for a shallow patch where there was an opportunity to overtake a large group of boats. Now Dick, like many other yachtsmen, knows exactly where to go and where not to go when it comes to sailing round the island. As the person in charge of all the Yachtmaster Ocean and Coastal Courses at the UKSA and a Yachtmaster Examiner himself he knows when and when not to push the boundaries, so he looked at me on the helm and said, "We will go for it." I asked whether he realised that if we put this boat on the bottom, the yachting press would have a field day with two 'Salties' on board. He just smiled and we over-sheeted both the mainsail and the genoa, put the boat over on her ear and slid across this sandbank overtaking at least 30 boats. I will not be doing that again in a hurry, Sir Francis must have been turning in his grave!

More recently I was asked to run a training programme for

Ian Atkins and his team, Rory Scott Dan Brown and Ben Field, the *Bam Bam* during their J70 programme covering the National Championships in Poole Bay and the World Championships in La Rochelle. They were another great team with many successes, especially in the upper wind range.

One of my scariest moments on the water was when I was taking their RIB from the River Hamble to Poole for the J70 Nationals. The weather forecast was for a fresh southerly wind which would be a reasonable crossing. However, when I arrived at the Needles it was blowing 40 knots and, looking across Christchurch Bay, it was not a pretty sight – I could see white water. I decided to hover inside Allum Bay for a while and wait for a moderation. Paul Hayes sailed past me in the J70 with just a storm jib up and was making progress so, as time was running out and I knew I was needed in Poole, I attempted a crossing. As I was approaching the Bridge Buoy I was completely swamped by a freak wave. Fortunately the big auto bailers kicked in and I accelerated and the water rushed back and over the transom and I returned to the safety of Allum Bay. Another hour passed with a slight moderation, so I decided to cross over to the mainland and then turn to the west and stay close in to the coast. This time I was successful, but it was still a rough ride and I arrived in Poole looking like a drowned ferret. The lads could not believe that I had done it and I told them that they had better win the event after that epic trip; they did, so it was all worthwhile in the end.

In my lifetime, as well as all the mates in the Royal Navy I spoke about, I also have made some long-standing friendships throughout my sailing career with whom I stay in close contact. In recent years I attended three reunions, one with the 420 class, one with the early members of the 470 class and another with the 505s, and it was so good to meet up again with such a great bunch of sailors.

I promised myself that when I retired, I would buy myself

a Jaguar XK convertible and I achieved this early on in my retirement and Christine and I have had many a pleasant holiday driving around Europe. We have driven to the northern, southern, eastern and western edges of mainland Europe and also England, Scotland and Wales and thoroughly enjoyed it. We celebrated our Golden Wedding Anniversary in June 2021 and, most importantly, we still have good health. Long may it continue!

SO THAT'S "MY LIFE IN A BLUE SUIT!"

Chapter 15

The Icing on the Cake

Just before this book went to print, I was told I was going to be awarded the **Lifetime Achievement Award** at the British Yachting Awards 2022 presented by *Sailing Today* with *Yachts & Yachting*. I have been sworn to secrecy until the ceremony, but the book has to go to print before then, so all we can put here is a brief mention.

I will be very proud to receive this award and my thanks go to *Sailing Today* with *Yachts & Yachting* and Chelsea Magazines.